Facilitating Team-Building Sessions: A Guide for Escape
Room and Exit Game Owners
By Christy M. Byrd, PhD
Copyright 2016 by Christy M. Byrd

Acknowledgements

Thank you to all the folks who made this possible, including my students and participants from over the years. Also thank you to the Facebook communities of escape room enthusiasts and owners for your questions, tips, and advice. Special thanks to my partner in life and business, Steven Cleek.

Facilitating Team-Building Sessions: A Guide for Escape
Room and Exit Game Owners
By Christy M. Byrd, PhD

Table of Contents

Introduction

If you're reading this, you already know that escape rooms are fun and interactive activities that require groups of teams to communicate and problem-solve together in order to be successful. This type of game is obviously suited for corporate groups and organizations as a team-building activity. According to a white paper by Scott Nicholson, 19% of escape room teams are corporate groups. But there's a lot more to team-building than having a group of people run through your escape room and having an open-ended discussion afterward. In this book you'll learn research-based strategies for designing and facilitating a rewarding team-building experience that will have your corporate customers returning again and again.

So what exactly is team building? In research on organizations, team building can refer to the general process through which teams learn to function effectively. Team building can occur at many levels. It can be a one-time, months' long process or be continuously integrated into the day-to-day functioning of an organization. As an escape room owner and not a consultant, you are not likely equipped to give organizations advice on the general functioning of their teams or to suggest major changes. Rather you are probably interested in, and this book is focused on, team building as a one-time meeting focused on set of activities that are designed to help a team accomplish a specific and narrow goal. That goal could be getting to know each other better, building skills, or resolving a conflict. Whatever the case, the group is calling on you for a limited amount of time and for a predetermined purpose. Ideally, they will receive insights about their particular goal, but an escape room team building session is unlikely to result in changes to an organization's structures, major processes, or products. This book will help you evaluate how your escape room can best serve a requesting organization, design a customized agenda, and facilitate a productive session.

I'm an escape room owner and psychologist. I received my PhD in education and psychology from the University of Michigan and have taught courses in educational psychology, developmental psychology, multicultural education, and research methods at three universities. Currently I'm teaching at the University of California, Santa Cruz, where I conduct research on school climate and intergroup relations. My training emphasized active learning and student engagement, and in all of my classes, large and small, I use interactive activities to get students to have fun learning and think at a deeper level.

In addition to my teaching experience, I have nine years of experience facilitating workshops for diverse groups. My workshop experience began as a graduate student, when I worked for the Program on Intergroup Relations at the University of Michigan. Our workshops focused on conflict resolution and increasing awareness of bias and prejudice. I also trained undergraduate student facilitators to lead intergroup dialogues on topics such as race, gender, and religion. At my current job in Santa Cruz, I run a research lab of thirty undergraduate and graduate students and offer workshops around campus on promoting a positive climate. In my years as a facilitator, I have learned how to plan effective workshops, how to address sensitive topics in a way that encourages learning, and how to deal with surprises from participants. In the first chapter of this book, I'll discuss what can happen when you get in front of a group without a plan. Then I'll share the four biggest challenges in facilitating team-building sessions: content, engagement, participants, and your facilitation style. The following chapters will cover each challenge in detail to give you the tools you need to design and carry out effective sessions.

If you have any feedback or want to talk more with me about how to increase corporate bookings for your escape room, send me an email at christy@exitsantacruz.com. I look forward to hearing from you!

The Problem with Bad Facilitation

Everyone has been in a training meeting that was boring, confusing, or just plain dumb. My most memorable experience was a diversity training for a job I had at a private tutoring center while I was in college. Our supervisor sat the eight employees, mostly college students, down in a conference room and, without much introduction, started playing a video. The video had a bored narrator voicing over terribly-acted scenes. The video tried to warn us of discrimination in the hiring process by showing an African American woman staidly interviewing a White man. In the next scene, the interviewer is speaking to another African American woman, and they share a sisterly laugh and fist-bump. Throughout, me and my co-workers are rolling our eyes and looking at the clock. We were already a racially diverse group that got along just fine. Why did we need to watch this video? The worst moment came when an African American man is talking to his White boss about a negative evaluation. Suddenly, out of nowhere, the terrible actor cries out, "It's because I'm gay, isn't it!" Me and my co-workers crack up with laughter. That was it for the session. Our supervisor tried to ask us some questions after the video, to no avail. All we could do was laugh and echo, "It's because I'm gay!" (Yes, we were dumb college students).

This is an example of team-building gone wrong. Poor planning, poor materials, and lack of engagement meant we didn't get anything out of that session. Ten years later, now having facilitated a hundred diversity trainings, I cringe to think about how terrible that session was. But I also feel sympathy for our poor supervisor, who hadn't produced that video and probably had no training in how to run that kind of training. You've probably been a part of other meetings and trainings that go wrong in other ways: they're boring, they devolve into sharing feelings with no real action, they create awkward moments, or worse, increase existing conflicts.

Being an escape room owner, you have the creativity and design capabilities to create fun and challenging puzzles. That does not necessarily mean you have the skills to manage the group dynamics within a team of strangers or to ensure that every person learns something. When you use an escape room as a team-building activity, you might have a few participants who dive right in and naturally draw conclusions about their own and their teammate's problem-solving abilities. These are probably current or future escape room enthusiasts and your target customers. But you will also have participants who will be bored, confused, or frustrated by the experience. At best, your bored participants will get nothing out of their time there. At worst, not only will they drag down the experience for everyone else, they'll complain about your business to everyone they know, not only losing you that corporate client but potentially driving away future customers.

So how do you ensure that all of your participants are engaged and want to come back for more? There are four major challenges to consider in facilitation, and in any learning experience, really. The first is creating **content**. You must have your goals in mind when designing your activities and structure the experience in such a way that everyone can reach those goals. But the room is already designed, you might be saying. How can I tailor it for every group and every person? You won't need to redesign your room for every client, but you can customize your pre-briefing and de-briefing sessions for maximum learning. In the next chapter I'll describe research on what in education we call *backwards design* to help you think about the content your team-building sessions will offer. I'll also describe what information to get from a requestor and a number of activities that you can use in your sessions, along with how they can help achieve different goals. Finally, I'll describe some assessments you can use to find your participants' strengths and weaknesses.

Second, you need strategies to promote **engagement**. Research is clear that *active learning* is preferred and results in better outcomes than sitting and passively listening to lectures. Escape rooms are inherently active, but I will share tips to ensure that most of your participants remain engaged throughout the session.

What happens when someone just doesn't want to cooperate? The third problem to consider is **disruptive participants.** There are many ways that participants can be disruptive, intentionally or not. I'll go over the types of disruption, the warning signs to watch out for, and give strategies for how to deal with conflict and return to a positive experience.

Finally, you need to consider your own **facilitation style**. Facilitation is more than standing in front of a group and having them do what you say. In order to engage an audience and have them trust you, you will need to be a *positive* and *authoritative* presence. But that looks different for each facilitator. I'll describe different facilitation styles and help you think about what works for you. I'll also talk about what to do when you as a facilitator get caught off guard or caught up in your own emotions and how to keep your own equilibrium. Last, you might not be facilitating alone, so I'll cover some important things to be aware of when working with a co-facilitator.

This book is aimed at escape room owners who don't have a lot of experience facilitating workshops or teaching, but I hope that even experienced professionals can draw some lessons more specific to the escape room experience. Of course, one book is not going to tell you everything you need to know about running successful team-building sessions. Experience with different groups is the best teacher. But this book will give you key points to consider in your planning and help you prepare for the unexpected.

Content: Designing a Great Experience

Characteristics of a High-Performing Team

What makes a successful team? We've all been in groups that don't work in some way or another. Sometimes it's the people—there's an egomaniac who has no flexibility in how things get done, or a slacker who doesn't contribute. Sometimes it's that the team doesn't have the skills or resources to get the work done. Sometimes it's that the team has no purpose or vision and really doesn't understand what they're supposed to do. Each of these teams will have a different set of problems and different goals to achieve in a team-building session. So the first aspect of designing great content for your team-building experiences is to understand what makes an effective team. According to research, high-performing teams have the "skills, attitudes, and competencies [that] enable them to achieve team goals. These team members set goals, make decisions, communicate, manage conflict, and solve problems in a supportive, trusting atmosphere in order to accomplish their objectives. Moreover, they are aware of their own strengths and weaknesses and have the ability to make changes when they need to improve their performance." (Dyer & Dyer, p.13)

Given this definition, it's possible to identify a set of key elements for a high-performing team. They can be organized in terms of thinking—the shared knowledge a group needs to have, doing—the tasks a team needs to be able to accomplish and the skills required to complete those tasks; and feeling—a team's cohesion and sense of connectedness (Salas & Cannon-Bowers, 1997).

- Think
    - Have clear goals
    - Have clear metrics for knowing when they meet their goals
    - Have clear processes in place
    - Understand each team member's roles and responsibilities
- Do
    - Make effective decisions
    - Communicate effectively
    - Resolve conflicts and disagreements effectively
    - Encourage risk-taking and innovation
    - Adapt to change over time
- Feel
    - Feel a sense of trust and commitment to the team and its goals

A team that has *clear goals* knows what it's doing. Goals are best when they are focused and concrete. For example, it's easier for someone to "write 10 pages" than to "work on chapter 2". You may have also heard the acronym SMART, which stands for Specific, Measureable, Attainable, Realistic, and Timely. Concrete goals require a clear understanding of the resources and processes involved, so a team-building session can help a group by providing space and structure to analyze what the ideal outcome is and how to get there.

Clear metrics are almost as important as clear goals. The best goals have metrics, such as "10 pages", built in. However, it may be useful to have several metrics for a particular goal and project. It's also important to understand who will be responsible for collecting and analyzing those metrics, which is part of the next goal, *clear processes.* All teams have a number of processes that determine how they work, and teams that have a good sense of who needs to do what when will work most efficiently. Finally in the "think" category is having a clear sense of *each team member's roles and responsibilities.* Teams require diverse skills and roles to function, and coordinating those roles requires forethought and communication.

Next, teams must *make effective decisions* on a day-to-day basis and for larger strategies. Teams that cannot decide or who have to constantly revisit decisions waste time, and teams that make the wrong decisions can cost the organization profits in addition to time. *Communicating effectively* is key to making decisions, as each team member must make their points of view clearly known. However, different viewpoints can lead to conflict, so teams must also learn to *resolve conflicts and disagreements* in ways that maintain team cohesion and help the team complete their work. Additionally, high-performing teams *encourage risk-taking and innovation,* they do not reproduce stale products. However, teams must feel efficacious and confident, as well as have high levels of creativity, to take on risks. The work context is not static, and high performing teams need to *adapt to change over time* as new challenges and opportunities arise. Finally, team cohesion is the foundation of a high-performing team. Teams that *feel a sense of trust and commitment* respect and encourage each other to do their best work. They are also invested in the goals of the team and fully committed to carrying out those goals.

Each of these elements can then be written as a goal for a team-building session. For example, a team that struggles with decision-making would have the learning objective of "improving decision-making capacity". In your meeting with the requestor, you will need to gather some details on what challenges the team is facing.

The Principle of Backward Design

Backward design is the idea of designing a learning experience with the end in mind. The "end" is your learning objectives, or what goals the team wants to achieve by the end of the session. You should be able to fit between one and four learning objectives in a few hours' session, depending on how many activities you have. Once you decide on your objectives, you select activities that will help you meet those objectives. If you have trouble thinking in terms of goals, think about the emotions and sensations you want participants to feel during the session. Should they feel a new sense of confidence? Do you want them to feel like they have a made a new friend of a co-worker? To feel less confused about what the team is doing? In the activity descriptions below, I describe particular overarching goals for each activity, but note that activities can meet multiple goals at the same time. For example, the goal of visioning is to help the team develop an idea of where they want to be, but the discussions involved will also help the participants get to know each other better and develop a sense of trust in the group. Thus, it's not necessary to choose one activity per learning objective. If you're not familiar with the activities I describe, the best way to understand what kinds of feelings are involved is to try them out yourself.

The Principle of Backward Design

Learning Objectives

Activities

Once you select your activities, you'll have the task of fitting them into your agenda. Generally, you will want to have a shorter block before the escape room and a longer block after. That way, the participants are still alert and awake when they go into the room. Their excitement about the experience will then sustain them for the later longer session. It's usually better to start with activities that are easy to get into and don't involve as much intensive thinking or personal risk before shifting into more in-depth activities. For example, participants may not be ready to jump into brainstorming at the very beginning of a session, before they've had a chance to feel comfortable with you and the space. A fun icebreaker or even just reviewing any assessments you've given allows time for the participants to warm up. I also don't recommend starting immediately with the escape room. You will want to spend at least a few minutes helping the participants understand what they should be looking for in the escape room and what to expect in the rest of the session.

You should also consider the way that excitement and energy shift over the course of the session. The factors that play into energy are how much participants are moving around and interacting with others. Individual writing and reflection is generally low energy. Small group discussions promote higher energy than a large group discussion because each person has a greater responsibility to speak. Large group discussions can be moderate to high energy if many people are participating but low energy if a few people dominate the conversation.

Generally, the escape room will be the most high-energy portion, so you can put your lowest energy activity immediately before. Keep the energy at a moderate level after the escape room with the discussion and activities following it. You won't want to crush the momentum and have the participants zone out for the rest of the session. You can capitalize on the energy from the escape room for the activity that will take the most intensive thinking. You can then allow the energy to fall throughout the end of the session and end with a low-energy activity. Alternatively, you could end with a very brief, high-energy activity so that participants leave remembering something fun. It's also useful to start out with a high or moderate energy activity to get participants to trust that the entire session won't be mind-numbing.

The length of the session will be determined by your business model or the requestor's needs. The shortest amount of time I recommend is half an hour after the escape room, which will allow for about ten minutes of discussion of the room, one activity based on the learning objectives, and a wrap-up. A longer amount of time will allow for an activity or two before the team goes into the room and another activity afterward. I would not recommend more than three or four hours in total because it is difficult to participants to maintain attention and commitment for so long. I've given some general time for each activity, but you can adjust them to fit your needs. Some, like brainstorming, are extremely flexible, while others, like active listening, require a more set amount of time.

As an example, for a two- or three-hour session, begin with simple introductions and/or a quick icebreaker. Give an overview of the day's activities and then set guidelines. Next, spend about twenty minutes on an opening activity. Conclude by preparing the team for the escape room. A restroom break is probably appropriate at this point. After the escape room, spend between twenty to minutes to an hour discussing the experience. Conduct one or two additional activities to solidify the learning objectives, and then conclude with a wrap-up activity.

Assessments is the final aspect of backward design. You can use assessments before the session to learn more about your participants, as I'll discuss later. You will also want to find out how well the learning objectives were met after the session. This can be done by giving the same assessments again, and measuring change, or simply by asking participants to describe the best and worst things about the session. I'll discuss getting feedback toward the end of this chapter.

Know Your Audience: Questions to Ask the Requestor

Now that you understand the importance of starting with learning objectives, let's go through the design of your team-building session and start with your first meeting with the requestor. You'll need to know some basic information about the team and their goals in order to best match your experience with what they are looking for. That includes the nature of the team, how it was formed, what its common tasks are, how many members it has, what are its major projects, goals, and deadlines, what existing roles there are, and what processes and evaluations are currently in place. It might be helpful to get an organizational chart and pictures of team members for reference during the session.

Once you understand the context of the team, you can ask specific questions to understand which necessary elements the team is weakest on and what are their goals for the session. You should start with a basic question like "What goals do you want to achieve?" However, some people are not great at describing their specific goals, or they might not have a clear idea of what they want. So here are some other questions you might ask to get clarity on that:

- Was there a troubling incident or conflict that occurred recently?
- How does the team get along?
- What are their major strengths as a team? Major weaknesses?
- Who are the major players in the group in terms of leadership and influence? How do others in the team feel about them?
- How do decisions get made in this team? Is everyone OK with that process?
- What behaviors would you like to see changed?
- What would you like to see happen differently in the team after this session?
- How would your ideal team function?

These questions are designed to get at how the team currently works and what improvements they could make. Requestors may be shy about airing "dirty laundry", so for some it might be best to keep your questions abstract and focused on ideals rather than reality. It is important, though, to get a little deeper than the initial request. Sometimes a requestor might describe an interpersonal conflict, but when you ask more questions you realize that the conflict is caused by a lack of vision and direction for the team. Your session can then be structured to meet both goals, for example, address the interpersonal conflict by having the team develop a mission statement. I would not necessarily suggest going through the list of key elements of a high-performing team above, since that might bring up issues the requestor had not thought of before. It's not possible to improve on all aspects of a team in a few hours' sessions, so it's best to let what's top-of-mind for the requestor drive the conversation. I recommend creating a preliminary list of 4-5 goals in your first meeting with the requestor, and let them know you will get back to them with a final list.

Once you have gathered information on what the team's goals are, do some further research on the company and its industry to get a sense of the types of people who usually work in it. This information will help you prepare activities that fit their skills and interests. For example, most social workers are women and have the motivation to help people who are struggling, so their session might focus more on the cooperative aspect of the escape room than a male-dominated tech start-up, where you might want to focus more on the feeling of challenge and beating the room. Of course, let the information in your research guide you more than rely on general stereotypes.

Know Your Rooms

Knowing your audience will allow you to match your escape room experience to the requestor's goals. For each of your rooms, you should make a list of the skills and capacities required to be successful in it. For example, is one room heavier on logic puzzles and cryptograms, while another has more physical challenges? What's the ideal number of people for each room? You should also think about the mood and emotional impact of each room that you offer. Are they scary, thrilling, or more light-hearted? A team attempting to overcome interpersonal conflict might benefit from the shared thrill of escaping from a zombie, but that same team might see a light-hearted room as trivializing their needs. Think about the high points of each room and how much they will meet the team's goals. For example, a team struggling with personal efficacy will benefit from rooms that allow individuals to experience small victories along the way. A team that is just getting to know each other might have a better experience with puzzles that require two or more people to work together at the same time. You can create a general document for your rooms so that when a team-building request comes in, you can see how your list of goals from your meeting with the requestor matches up. As you assess your rooms, you may need to add to or modify the original set of goals. As noted, it's important to be upfront with the requestor about what your experience can and cannot offer. Your rooms are probably already aimed at a variety of skills, but if you have the time and energy, you may consider modifying a few puzzles in content or form especially for this group. The modification could be as simple as substituting the organization's name somewhere or designing a custom puzzle to suit the organization's needs.

Since the room can only offer a limited experience, the most customization will occur in your pre-briefing and de-briefing discussions. The next three sections will explore activities and assessments to use for meeting different types of goals. The tables below give a cross-listing for each learning goal and activity so that you can find them quickly. These are suggestions based on my experience. Feel free to adapt the activities and assessments for what you think fits each team. Once you have selected a set of activities, put together a preliminary agenda and discuss it with your requestor.

Learning Objective	Suggested Activities	Suggested Assessments
Have clear goals	Goal-setting Task analysis Visioning	Goal orientation

Have clear metrics for knowing when they meet their goals	Brainstorming Task analysis Visioning	Goal orientation
Have clear processes in place	Brainstorming Influence line Task analysis	Goal orientation Self-efficacy
Understand each team member's roles and responsibilities	Active listening Influence line Task analysis Visioning	Goal orientation Personality Self-efficacy
Make effective decisions	Active listening LARA Task analysis	Conflict resolution style Self-efficacy
Communicate effectively	Active listening LARA	Conflict resolution style Personality Self-efficacy Sense of

		community
Resolve conflicts and disagreements effectively	Active listening Influence line LARA	Conflict resolution style Mindset Sense of community
Encourage risk-taking and innovation	Brainstorming Task analysis Visioning	Mindset Self-efficacy
Adapt to change over time	Goal setting Timeline Visioning	Mindset
Feel a sense of trust and commitment to the team and its goals	Active listening Concentric circles Goal setting Timeline Visioning	Sense of community

Activity	Possible Learning Objectives
Active Listening	Understand roles and responsibilities

	Make effective decisions
	Communicate effectively
	Feel a sense of trust and commitment
	Resolve conflicts effectively
Brainstorming	Have clear metrics
	Have clear processes
	Encourage risk-taking and innovation
Concentric Circles	Feel a sense of trust and commitment
Goal Setting	Have clear goals
	Feel a sense of trust and commitment
	Adapt to change over time
Influence Line	Have clear processes
	Understand roles and responsibilities
	Resolve conflicts effectively
LARA	Make effective decisions
	Communicate effectively
	Resolve conflicts effectively
Task Analysis	Have clear goals
	Have clear metrics

	Have clear processes Understand roles and responsibilities Make effective decisions Encourage risk-taking and innovation
Timeline	Feel a sense of trust and commitment Adapt to change over time
Visioning	Have clear goals Have clear metrics Understand roles and responsibilities Feel a sense of trust and commitment Encourage risk-taking and innovation Adapt to change over time

Activities to Use

Setting guidelines. It is essential that every group set guidelines for positive communication before beginning any in-depth discussions. Guidelines help participants feel comfortable sharing their views and remain open to learning.

Ask participants to generate a list or present the sample guidelines below and ask for modifications or additions. Make sure the participants feel that the guidelines are jointly created and/or agreed upon. This will increase the chance that participants follow them.

Sample guidelines:

- Everyone should have the chance to share; everyone has the responsibility to share
- Trust that everyone is doing the best they can (give the benefit of a doubt)
- Challenge the idea, not the person (focus on the content of what has been said, not on attacking the person who said it)
- What is said here, stays here

Post the guidelines in a visible place. Encourage participants to remind each other of the guidelines if necessary and tell the participants that you may call attention to the guidelines if you feel they are not being followed.

Discussing the escape room. When you discuss the escape room, it is usually easiest to have participants first share their general impressions in the large group and then ask specific questions to drill down into different aspects of their experiences. Most people will naturally be excited and want to go over what happened; however, you will want to limit this open sharing to five or ten minutes so that you can focus the group on their learning objectives. If the group is reluctant to share in the large group, start in small groups of three or four to help participants feel more comfortable. If participants were divided up in some way (for example, in two different prison cells) it might be useful to have members of one group describe what it was like for their side and then have members of the other group share so that everyone can have a common understanding of the room. If you do a walkthrough of your escape rooms, you can do it immediately after the team finishes the room or go through each puzzle in the discussion and have the team analyze their performance.

Some specific questions to ask are: Who solved X puzzle? What was your process? What was your goal when you were doing X? How did you figure out X? How did you make decisions? How was conflict handled? What patterns did you notice in how your team worked together? I noticed X happened; what was going on there? What did you do well? What could you have done better? Did you personally feel like you contributed? What a barrier to your participation? Who was "checked-out" or didn't contribute as much, and why? How does what happened in the room relate to how you work in the real world? What lessons can you take away?

It is important to realize that during the discussion you are not just rehashing everything that happened. Your task as the facilitator is the lead the group in drawing generalizable lessons from their experience in the room that can be applied to their work together. For example, if Ashley was able to solve a word puzzle in the room, ask her co-workers how she shows that skill at work. Her co-workers can bring up examples of her verbal abilities that they are aware of, showing appreciation for her, or they might comment that they don't usually see that skill. The latter would provide the opportunity for the team to reflect on whether Ashley feels she's being underutilized at work or simply allow for a newfound sense of respect.

Note that not every moment in the game needs to be talked over. As the facilitator who is aware of the team's challenges and goals, you will want to draw attention to the patterns and moments that will best meet those goals. For teams that need to work on interpersonal conflict or getting to know each other, highlight moments of successful joint effort and shared emotions. For teams that need help with communication or decision-making, highlight moments of problem-solving process. Of course, you should also allow for the team to bring up revelations that are meaningful for them, as well.

This discussion can last from twenty minutes to an hour. For discussions that last closer to an hour, be sure to have a variety of questions, to cover the breadth of the room experience, and to give everyone a chance to talk. For shorter discussions, it's not necessary that everyone talk or that you cover the entire room experience—focus on the moments most relevant to the team's goals. The discussion can be integrated into or used to transition to other activities.

Active listening (Materials: none; Time: 60 minutes). The objective of this activity is for participants to practice their listening skills. Have team members sit in groups of three (four is OK) with the instruction sheet in Appendix A. One person is the speaker, one is the listener, and one (or two) is the observer. The speaker should talk for five minutes on the prompt, while the listener and observer(s) are silent. The listener can nod or show that they are listening, but they should not say anything. Then, for three or four minutes, the listener should say what they heard. This is the opportunity for the listener to repeat back what the speaker said, not to tell their own stories or respond to what the listener said. In the next five minutes, the observer should comment on what they saw in the speaker and listener's non-verbal behavior and what they themselves heard in the conversation. They should comment on how accurate the listener's summary of what the talker said was.

Rotate roles that so everyone has a chance to be the speaker, listener, and observer. When everyone has been in each role, spend about fifteen minutes debriefing the activity. What did they notice about themselves and others? What did they learn? Did they become more aware of the importance of listening carefully? How did it feel to remain silent? What was it like to receive feedback?

Sample prompts can focus on participants' lives growing up, their goals and passions, what they like about their work or the organization, or their hobbies outside of work. You should select prompts that are aligned with the learning objectives. For example, for a conflict resolution session, a prompt could ask participants how their family dealt with conflict when they were growing up. For a team that needs help making decisions, you could prompt participants to discuss a recent problem they had to solve. Prompts should be personal enough that participants feel they have something meaningful to share; however, prompts should not be so intimate that participants feel uncomfortable or threatened by sharing. When discussing childhood experiences, focus on fairly general and universal concepts (e.g., family or school life, favorite things) that allow participants to choose how deeply they want to share rather than particular relationships or situations (e.g., relationship with a parent).

This activity is best suited for before the escape room because participants will have the opportunity to immediately practice their new listening skills. However, you might also place this activity after the escape room and have the prompt focus on the escape room experience so that every participant gets to deeply reflect on the team's performance.

Brainstorming. (Materials: whiteboard or pen and paper; Time: 10-60 minutes). Brainstorming is a basic activity suitable for most learning objectives and before or after the escape room. The structure requires identifying a prompt and having participants generate ideas for the prompt. As facilitator, you have a great deal of freedom in guiding participants' ideas to ensure that the team's learning objectives are met.

Concentric circles. (Materials: none; Time: 20 minutes). The goal of this activity is for participants to get to know each other better. Unlike the timeline activity described later, where participants are in pairs or triads, participants will get to talk with at least five or six others. Have participants stand in two concentric circles. The inner circle should be facing outward and the outer circle facing inward.

Make sure each participant is facing just one other person. Have the participants discuss the prompt for three minutes, and then have the outer circle rotate so that each person is facing someone new. Give a new prompt, allow time for discussion, and rotate another four or five times. Rotate fewer times or use briefer prompts to shorten this activity.

Some sample prompts are: Why did your parents name you what they did? What do you do for fun? What's your favorite thing about work? What's your biggest challenge at work? Where do you see yourself in five years? The prompts can be anything, from trivial to philosophical, as the main goal is for participants to share one-on-one. This allows time to discuss topics that may not usually come up in the workplace and for participants to talk with co-workers they may not usually see. This activity can be integrated into other activities and structured to meet almost any objective as well. For example, individuals can share their goals for the team one-on-one, and then discuss goals in the large group.

This activity does not need to be discussed in the large group. It is ideal for early in the session before transitioning into weightier activities.

Goal setting. (Materials: a sheet of paper for each team member, a whiteboard; Time: at least 20 minutes). The objective is to get the group to set some goals. The trick is that through this process the team will realize how much they are in agreement (or not!) about what they're looking for. By the end of the activity, everyone will better understand the group's values and objectives. Even if everyone does not agree with the goals, they will be able to understand everyone's point of view and appreciate that the process the group went through.

Start this activity by having the team leader describe the basic context of the group. Even if you have this information from the requestor, it's good for you to hear again and for the group to start with safe, commonly known material. Importantly, make sure the team leader does *not* say what their goal for the group is. This could influence the team members to simply agree without exploring their own thoughts. You as the facilitator might also emphasize the need for goals that are concrete and measurable.

Then, have team members individually write down what they think the team's goals should be. Everyone should contribute at this stage so that they feel they had a voice in the process. Only give a few minutes and don't allow questions or discussion yet. If the team has been struggling with goal-setting, it's likely that every person has already thought at least some about what they are supposed to be doing. If people are struggling at this stage, have them write down what they *don't* want the goals to be.

Once everyone has a list, have the team get together in small groups of three to five people to discuss what they came up with. Have the small groups note where they agree and try to understand the context of, if not resolve, disagreements. Each small group should come up with two lists: one set of agreed-upon goals, and another set of questions/concerns to raise with the large group.

Start the large group discussion with the agreed-upon goals. You're likely to find that each group has similar things they agreed on. Write these on the white board so that the team can see their progress and feel a sense of collective efficacy. If nothing else, they can leave with some common objectives. Next start going through the questions and concerns, and take notes on the whiteboard. This is where your skill as a facilitator will come into play. Make sure everyone understands the points of disagreement, the stakes (is this something we need to decide right now or can we table it for six months?), and the decision-making process. For example, it may not be useful to debate whether deciding on product color should be a goal of the group when ultimately a separate design team will make that decision. You're not likely to get through every point of disagreement, but the process of discussing the disagreements out loud will help everyone in the group understand what the different positions are so that they are prepared for future conversations.

End this activity by summarizing the discussion and re-emphasizing the agreed-upon goals that the team came up with. Ask the group if they are willing to commit to those goals today by raising their hand or calling out "Yes!" to feel a sense of solidarity.

The escape room can be done before or after this activity. Have participants do the escape room before to create a sense of urgency about the need to agree on the team's purpose. As you analyze what happened in the room, you can highlight where having clear goals would have been helpful. Having participants do the escape room after this activity can solidify the sense of collaboration that emerged during the goal-setting and possibly show those who disagreed with each other that their conflicts do not have to detract from the overall success of the team.

Influence line. (Materials: none; Time 15-30 minutes). The goal of this activity is to help participants reflect on how power is distributed in the group. Many groups have a nominal power structure, but power may play out along other lines, such as outspokenness, years of experience, or gender. This activity should be done after the escape room. Have the participants stand up and silently get into a line from most influential to least influential, based on their work in the escape room. The participants should place themselves first and then think about their relationship to other participants. They can move each other around, but all of the interactions must be silent. Don't allow the participants to spend too much time or effort moving other people around.

When the participants have had a few minutes to get into a line, ask them to look around for a few seconds and reflect on their position and the position of others. Then begin debriefing by asking questions such as

- How do you feel about where you are?
- How did you define influence when thinking about placement?
- How did you decide where to place yourself?
- Who did you try to move and why?
- For those who were moved, how did it feel to have a different perception of your influence?

Allow participants to disagree on who has more or less influence and why. It's not necessary to resolve those conflicts—remind participants that people have different perceptions and that's OK. The second stage of the debrief should focus on how the influence line translates to their normal work environment. Sometimes, the most influential will be the nominal or actual leaders at work. Alternatively, new leaders could emerge because the escape room experience is so different from their normal work roles. Based on the team's objectives, try to get the participants to generate takeaways. Is the team interested in balancing power? Then have the most influential people acknowledge ways they can share power with others and the least influential think about how to step up. Are the least influential dissatisfied and feeling unheard? Have the group reflect on ways that everyone can contribute feedback even if actual power cannot be shared.

Note that the influence line can bring up powerful emotions. People in the United States, at least, view themselves as living in an egalitarian society. Thus, paying explicit attention to power may be uncomfortable and threatening to a wide variety of people. It's not necessary to push quiet participants to talk in this activity because they may be feeling emotional or afraid of consequences outside of the session if they speak. Remind the team of the guidelines they set at the beginning of the session and that the goal is for everyone to learn from this experience. Pay particular attention to nonverbal cues and facial expressions to determine whether anyone is getting too upset. If that occurs or the group is reluctant to talk, don't be afraid to take a break or ask the participants to spend a few minutes writing on their own before coming back to the large group.

As mentioned, it's best to do the influence line after the escape room, but you might consider doing two lines, one before and one after. In the first line, the participants will organize themselves based on their perceived work roles, and the line after will challenge or confirm their assumptions.

LARA. (Materials: handout; Time: 10 minutes). LARA is a technique developed by the organization Love Makes a Family to help individuals respond to hostile comments. LARA stands for Listen, Affirm, Respond, and Add Information. *Listen* calls on active listening skills and asks the responder to identify the beliefs and emotions that lie at the core of the statement. *Affirming* has the responder identify any small piece of what has been said that they can agree with. That can be a feeling (I'm frustrated, too), a belief (I want what's best for the team), or a principle. This can promote positive feelings and help the antagonist understand that the responder is trying to be reasonable. *Respond* is where the responder answers the question raised or gives their perspective on the issue. It's important that the respond section is a direct response and not a misdirection onto another topic. Finally, the responder *adds information,* such as by raising a new way of thinking about the issue. This is the opportunity to change the topic slightly. There is a handout that summarizes LARA in Appendix A.

Since LARA is more of a tool than an activity, you can introduce it and then have participants practice with prompts or move on to another activity. LARA can be used before or after the escape room. Before, it can help participants feel that they have been given a very specific skill to use during the rest of the session. The discussion after the escape room can then focus on other skills or give them the chance to use LARA in the discussion. Teaching LARA early on is especially good if conflict between two people or over a certain issue led to the request for the session because it will set the stage for the discussion. Teaching LARA after the escape room may be beneficial if the requestor feels that other objectives, such as setting goals, are more pressing. Having LARA as the last activity could also be useful if many of the participants are resistant to the idea of team-building. The specific skill learned will be the last thing they remember, so it will be hard for them to say they didn't get anything out of the session!

Task analysis. (Materials: paper and pen and/or whiteboard; Time: at least 20 minutes). The goal of this activity is to have participants clarify what is necessary to complete a specific project. It is possible that the team has engaged in this type of activity at some point, however, you might be surprised by how many groups set off on projects without understanding the resources and procedures necessary to complete it. You can get a sense of this from the requestor meeting.

This activity can be done in the large group, although you can break into smaller groups if the team gets stuck or if individuals feel their roles are too disparate. Make sure to spend some time in the large group as well to make sure the pieces fit together. List the end goal first, and then list all of the resources and tasks necessary for that goal to be reached. Allow for lots of space between these items. Then go through each resource and sub-task and list the resources and tasks necessary for those to be completed. Continue this until you run out of space or have broken each task down to a sufficient level of detail (what is sufficient will depend on the specific task). At this point, you might want to transfer the list to another board or rewrite it in a neater form.

Next, have the team distinguish between resources that already exist and those that will need to be created. Add new tasks for those resources that need to be created. Then have the team discuss the tasks, such as which tasks are absolutely essential, which they have the capacity to do, which they need to develop the capacity to do. They may want to discuss timelines at this point or wait until the analysis is more complete. The group may want to begin assigning individuals to tasks or create a list of action points for their next team meeting. Ideally, this activity will reveal steps in the process that have been overlooked or assumptions team members have made about responsibilities. As facilitator, drive the group toward making easy decisions but emphasize that it is not necessary to nail down every detail right now. When you reach a stopping point, have the group step back and reflect on the activity as a whole. Some questions to ask are: What did you realize in this activity? What questions will you take back to your organization? What were some benefits of doing this activity? What new perspectives do you have on your role?

This activity can be used before the escape room to help a newly-formed group achieve clarity and solidarity. The de-brief can then highlight how the team's effective problem-solving and communication in the escape room can be applied to their project. This can give a sense of energy and excitement for the next phase of work. Alternatively, you can use this activity after the escape room and call on the participants to treat the task analysis like another puzzle. The participants may have more creative ways of thinking through roadblocks or about the meaning of collaboration after having done the escape room, especially if the room uses very different skills than the participants use in their day-to-day work.

Timeline. (Materials: paper and pen; Time: 30 minutes). This activity helps participants get to know each other and clarify their personal ambitions. Have participants create a timeline of their career, starting either from their first job in the field or when they first joined this particular organization. They should highlight milestones or especially significant moments. Then, they should list three personal goals for the next five to ten years. This should take about five to ten minutes. Then have participants share their timelines in pairs or triads for about fifteen minutes. Participants might know basic facts about their co-workers, but this activity should reveal new details or fun insights. Spend a few minutes debriefing by asking participants to share any surprises in the large group.

This activity is best suited for doing before the escape room. Participants are likely to work more closely with their partners from the activity once they get into the room and create bonds that will last outside of the session.

Visioning. (Materials: laptops or magazines, posterboards, and craft supplies; Time: 40 minutes). In this activity, participants will create a vision board and imagine an ideal future. Visualization is a useful skill, as psychologists have found that it helps people to have a more positive outlook and to be more persistent in achieving their goals. Athletes use visualization to mentally prepare for the actions they will take in their sport—this same sort of mental exercise can be useful for daily situations as well. Additionally, through this activity the team will work to build a shared vision—ideally the conversations that emerge as they create and discuss their boards will give all a firmer sense of purpose. Encourage the team to hang their boards in a prominent place back at work.

There is an example instruction sheet in Appendix A. First, have participants work in small groups of 3 to 6 to create their board virtually using images from the internet or on a piece of posterboard with magazines. Give the team a prompt such as "What is your vision for this team/organization?" After about 20 minutes, have each group come up and describe their vision board. Then discuss in the large group for about 10 minutes what the team noticed about their visions, what commonalities there were and what differences came up. This activity might seem hokey to some, but by the end most will likely appreciate the opportunity to image an ideal future with their teammates and commit to building it. Additionally, the more artsy and hands-on members of the team will enjoy using a skill that may be less on display in their day-to-day jobs.

Use this activity before the escape room to have the team feel a sense of connection to each other before taking on a shared challenge. It may not work as well after an escape room because participants may be more interested in analyzing their performance and the team as it works now rather than an abstract future. Nevertheless, visioning may be useful after completing the escape room to help the team focus on how they want to improve.

Wrapping up. No session will ever feel complete, but it is important to end sessions with some sense of closure and, ideally, hope and excitement for the future. Some ways to end the session are:

One-word go-around: Have each participant say one word about how they're feeling or what they got out of the session.

Thank-you's: Have each participant find at least one person to thank for something that happened during the session, whether it was an insight or help with a puzzle in the escape room.

Tomorrow I will: Have each participant write down their immediate next step, based on what they learned in the session. They can share their steps with teammates to ensure accountability.

What we learned: Have each participant list one thing they learned from the session. Put the lessons on a shared document that the team can display in their office.

Should you have the group do multiple escape rooms? I don't think an effective team-building session requires multiple escape room experiences. Although doing two rooms in one day may be fun for the budding enthusiasts, for many it will require the same skills they have already used in the first room. Your participants will be looking for ways to generalize their experience to their work responsibilities, and some of the other activities in this chapter are better suited to that. An additional downside to having the team do multiple escape rooms is that you are reducing the potential that the participants will return on their own as paying customers.

Using Assessment Tools

Assessment tools can be useful for helping you understand the group and for giving the group information about itself. While many people are aware of their strengths and weaknesses, assigning a quantitative score to yourself and seeing how you compare with your co-workers can be eye-opening. There are thousands of surveys available on the internet for you to use, but in this book I have selected a handful based on the types of traits and characteristics I've found most useful in my team-building experiences. The items are below and in Appendix B. Feel free to mix and match.

Ideal assessments should be relatively short and easy to score (unless you have access to an automatic scoring system). They should also have some degree of "face validity" but not be too simplistic. Face validity means that the content of the items, at face value, seems to fit with the constructs being measured. There are some scales constructed that are valid without necessarily having face validity, but most non-technicians feel most comfortable with tools that are intuitive. Additionally, you will not want to spend too much time during the session explaining and justifying your assessments. At the same time, your assessments will not be taken seriously if they feel like they came from a magazine or quiz website. Aim for scales with content that may not be immediately obvious just from looking at the items but that are intuitive once participants understand the scoring. Of course, I recommend using scales that have a strong research base as well!

There are several ways to incorporate assessment tools into your session. You can use them as informational resources, both to help you plan the session and for the team to reflect on their capacities individually and as a group. It is not necessary to discuss the results in depth during the session, and some assessments, such as the one for sense of community, may be more appropriate for team members to review one-on-one or at other times. However, in most cases, you will want to draw some attention to the way individuals' and the group's scores played out in the escape room.

You can also use the review of assessments as an activity. Have participants look at their scores and discuss what is interesting and surprising. Then have participants identify an area they want to pay attention to or work on while in the escape room. During the escape room discussion, ask participants whether they met their personal goal. You might also have the participants complete the assessments after the escape room, focused on the experience within the room. These experience-specific scores can then be discussed on their own or compared to the assessments taken before the escape room. For example, if someone is extrinsically motivated for work but was intrinsically motivated in the escape room, why might that be? Are there ways to make work more intrinsically motivating, or is it OK to have the different types of motivation because the skills required are so different?

Another way to use assessment tools as an activity is to have participants take the assessment and then divide up into groups based on their dominant style (for example, those with more of an fixed mindset in one group and those with more of a growth mindset in another group). Have the groups discuss the advantages and disadvantages of their style while taking notes. Each group should present on "how to understand us" to the other group. Then have a large group discussion about how the styles can work together effectively.

Finally, it's important to note that survey scales are not perfect measurements. Have participants identify the ways the assessments match them but don't be afraid if participants raise concerns about how the score may not fit, or may not fit in certain situations. Lead the discussion toward the varying circumstances, with the goal of still drawing some general conclusions about the person's or group's behavior. Emphasize that the assessments are tools to aid in the team's learning, and it's up to the participants to take what they can from the experience. Put it back on the participants to reflect on what they can learn.

You can download the assessment tools described below at http://www.exitsantacruz.com/team-building-book/.

Conflict resolution style. Interpersonal conflict is caused when there is a threat to someone's goals or self-esteem. Organizational psychologists have identified five ways that employees deal with conflict with other people classified along two dimensions: how much one attempts to meet their own needs and how much one tries to accommodate the needs of others. A person with the *avoiding* style has low concern for self and the other person in the conflict, so they will withdraw from the conflict. This makes them unassertive but also uncooperative. They may preserve relationships during a conflict but the conflict may remain unresolved. A person with the *obliging* style has low concern for the self and high concern for others, so they will downplay their needs to accommodate the other person. The obliging person often ends up in a win-lose situation, with them losing out. Someone with the *dominating* style, on the other hand, will place their needs over the needs of others. People with this style are focused on goals over relationships and may not hesitate to use aggressive behavior—this can make them uncooperative and threatening. This style can be effective for getting decisions made, but it can create resentment toward those who are dominated.

The *integrating* style describes those who have high concern for themselves and the other person in the conflict.

They attempt to use a high level of collaboration and openness to meet everyone's needs. This style can be effective at helping everyone get what they want but requires a great deal of time and effort to build consensus. A fifth style involves a moderate level of concern for both parties and attempts to reach a mutual compromise. This is known as the *compromising* style. The compromising style is effective at preserving relationships but is not as time-consuming as a fully integrative style. However, since not everyone can have their needs met, the outcome may not be ideal.

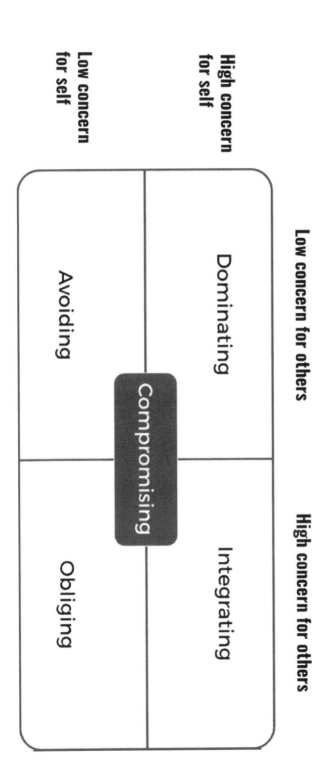

Conflict Resolution Styles

High concern
for self

Low concern
for self

Low concern for others

High concern for others

Dominating

Avoiding

Compromising

Integrating

Obliging

57

Dominating and avoiding styles are associated with worse work relationships and subsequent performance, whereas collaboration is associated with the better performance. The impact of conflict style is also based on the context, however. The dominant style is useful when the team is stuck or when the need for a decision is urgent and maintaining supportive relationships is not critical. In some situations, a group may need someone to take charge and solve a problem. The avoiding style can be useful when the issue is trivial and confrontation would cause more harm than good, or when others could more successfully resolve the conflict. The obliging style can be appropriate when the relationship is the highest priority. This is also an appropriate time to use the integrating style. This style is also effective when time is not a concern and building consensus will create commitment and buy-in from team members. Finally, the compromising style is useful for complex issues with no simple solution and when the people involved in the conflict have equal levels of power.

Clearly, a conflict resolution assessment can be used for teams that are experiencing interpersonal struggles. It may be useful to have participants go over their scores early in the team-building session. After the escape room and the other activities, they can reflect on how their behavior fits the scores and what changes they might want to make. It is most useful to present the assessment as the starting point for discussion rather than as a diagnosis. Since conflict resolution style is more of a personality variable, participants may be resistant to the message that they need to change. Instead, you can use the session to help participants think through when they should consider a different approach. There is a conflict resolution style handout in Appendix A.

Rahim Organizational Conflict Inventory–II (Rahim, 1983)

1.   I try to investigate an issue with my peers to find a solution acceptable to us.

2.   I generally try to satisfy the needs of my peers.

3.   I attempt to avoid being "put on the spot" and try to keep my conflict with my peers to myself.

4.   I try to integrate my ideas with those of my peers to come up with a decision jointly.

5.   I try to work with my peers to find solution to a problem that satisfies our expectations.

6.   I usually avoid open discussion of my differences with my peers.

7.   I try to find a middle course to resolve an impasse.

8.	I use my influence to get my ideas accepted.

9.	I use my authority to make a decision in my favor.

10.	I usually accommodate the wishes of my peers.

11.	I give in to the wishes of my peers.

12.	I exchange accurate information with my peers to solve a problem together.

13.	I usually allow concessions to my peers.

14.	I usually propose a middle ground for breaking deadlocks.

15.	I negotiate with my peers so that a compromise can be reached.

16.	I try to stay away from disagreement with my peers.

17.	I avoid an encounter with my peers.

18.	I use my expertise to make a decision in my favor.

19.	I often go along with the suggestions of my peers.

20.	I use "give and take" so that a compromise can be made.

21.	I am generally firm in pursuing my side of the issue.

22.	I try to bring all our concerns out in the open so that the issues can be resolved in the best possible way.

23.	I collaborate with my peers to come up with decisions acceptable to us.

24.	I try to satisfy the expectations of my peers.

25.   I sometimes use my power to win a competitive situation.

26.   I try to keep my disagreement with my peers to myself in order to avoid hard feelings.

27.   I try to avoid unpleasant exchanges with my peers.

28.   I try to work with my peers for a proper understanding of a problem.

Scoring: Take the average of each set of items—Integrating: 1, 4, 5, 12, 22, 23, 28; Obliging: 2, 10, 11, 13, 19, 24; Dominating: 8, 9, 18, 21, 25; Avoiding: 3, 6, 16, 17, 26, 27; Compromising: 7, 14, 15, 20.

Goal orientation. Goal orientation refers to a person's motivation for engaging in an activity. The idea was developed initially by educational psychologist Carol Midgely and her colleagues. There are two primary orientations: mastery and performance. Those with a mastery goal orientation work on a task because they want to master it. They need to feel a sense of competency and are intrinsically motivated. They love what they are doing and they are unlikely to give up in the face of challenges. The possibility of failure isn't a deterrent.

On the other hand, those with a performance goal orientation are more extrinsically motivated—they work on a task because they want to look good (or they want to avoid looking incompetent). For them, the reward comes the praise and recognition they get from finishing. This can be a great motivator, but compared to those with mastery goal orientations, those with performance goal orientations are more likely to give up or not even try if something seems too challenging.

Both types of goal orientations can be useful in different circumstances. It is useful to understand individuals' goal orientations in order to structure goals and rewards. For example, a mastery-oriented person may not be as interested in a competitive system, whereas a performance-oriented person might thrive in that system.

Goal orientation assessments can be useful in a variety of situations. Use it before having teams set goals or assign responsibilities so that group members can find a good fit. For example, the performance-oriented team member might be better suited for presenting the project to supervisors, whereas a mastery-oriented team member could be a better fit for handling revisions. Understanding the goal orientations of their teammates might also help groups that are not fitting together well or that have conflicts over processes and outcomes. Knowing what they as individuals value can help the group come to agreement about what they jointly value.

Goal Orientation Scale (Button, Mathieu & Zajac, 1996)

1. The opportunity to do challenging work is important to me.

2. When I fail to complete a difficult task, I plan to try harder the next time I work on it.

3. I prefer to work on tasks that force me to learn new things.

4. The opportunity to learn new things is important to me.

5. I do my best when I'm working on a fairly difficult task.

6. I try hard to improve on my past performance.

7. The opportunity to extend the range of my abilities is important to me.

8. When I have difficulty solving a problem, I enjoy trying different approaches to see which one will work.

9. I prefer to do things that I can do well rather than things that I do poorly.

10. I'm happiest at work when I perform tasks on which I know that I won't make any errors.

11. The things I enjoy the most are the things I do the best.

12. The opinions others have about how well I do certain things are important to me.

13. I feel smart when I do something without making any mistakes.

14. I like to be fairly confident that I can successfully perform a task before I attempt it.

15. I like to work on tasks that I have done well on in the past.

16. I feel smart when I can do something better than most other people.

Scoring: Take the average of items 1-8 for the mastery goal orientation score, and the average of items 9-16 for the performance goal orientation score.

Mindset. Mindset refers to how people think about the nature of ability and intelligence. The construct is based on the research of learning theorist Carol Dweck. Those with an fixed mindset believe that people are given a certain amount to start out with, and you can't change it much. Those with this type of belief interpret failure as information that maybe you don't have what it takes to be successful. Those with a growth or incremental mindset, in contrast, believe that ability and intelligence is malleable. You may start out at a certain level, but with effort you can become better. For these individuals, failure is feedback about where you need to improve. Mindsets have implications for how much people persist when they face challenges. If something is difficult and you just don't have what it takes, why not just give up? But if you believe it's possible to grow your skills, you might be more willing to try again later. Research has shown that it's possible to shift people's mindsets toward growth, with positive results for perseverance.

Use the mindset assessment to diagnose teams with interpersonal conflicts or that are struggling to overcome challenges. Team members who differ in mindset might conflict over how to handle a problem, so understanding the different points of view can allow the group to focus on their actual resources and capacities and jointly decide how to continue. The mindset assessment can also be valuable if there is consistent conflict between team members and a team leader. A team leader who has a different mindset from the team members could use inappropriate reward structures. For example, if a team member mentions a problem with a task, an fixed-minded team leader might assign the team member to a different task instead of giving them more resources to work out the problem, which is what the growth-minded team member would prefer.

Mindset (adapted from Dweck, 2000)

1.   Everyone has certain amount of ability and we can't really do much to change it.

2.   People's ability is something about they that they can't change very much.

3.   No matter who someone is, he/she can significantly change his/her ability level.

4.   To be honest, people can't really change how capable they are.

5.   People can always substantially change how capable they are.

6.   Someone can learn new things, but he/she can't really change his/her basic intelligence.

7.   No matter how much intelligence people have, everyone can always change it quite a bit.

8.   Everyone can change even their basic ability level considerably.

Scoring: Take the average of items 1, 2, 4, and 6 for fixed mindset and items 3, 5, 7, and 8 for growth mindset.

Personality. Personality can play a role in how people communicate and resolve conflicts. There are several major models of personality that measure individuals on various dimensions of personality. One is called the Big Five or the Five Factor Model and it includes these traits:

- **Extraversion:** How outgoing someone is
- **Agreeableness:** How kind, sympathetic, and affectionate someone is
- **Conscientiousness:** Includes organization, planfulness, and attention to detail
- **Neuroticism:** How tense, anxious, and emotional stable someone is
- **Openness to Experience:** How much someone has wide interests and is imaginative and insightful

Most people will not be surprised by their scores on a Big Five personality assessment. This assessment tool is most useful as a way to describe the overall character of a team and to help team members think through how to be effective with diverse personalities. Personality is very stable over time and most people are not interested in changing their personality. Therefore, I would suggest using assessments that measure motivation, like goal orientation, mindset, and self-efficacy, in addition to a personality assessment. A short measure of personality is included below. Longer versions can be found on the internet.

Ten Item Personality Measure (Gosling, et al., 2003)

1. Extraverted, enthusiastic.

2. Critical, quarrelsome.

3. Dependable, self-disciplined.

4. Anxious, easily upset.

5. Open to new experiences, complex.

6. Reserved, quiet.

7. Sympathetic, warm.

8. Disorganized, careless.

9. Calm, emotionally stable.

10. Conventional, uncreative.

Scoring: Reverse the items marked with an R so that 1 = 5, 2 = 4, 3 = 3, 4 = 2, and 5 = 1. Then take the average of both items. Extraversion: 1, 6R; Agreeableness: 2R, 7; Conscientiousness; 3, 8R; Emotional Stability: 4R, 9; Openness to Experiences: 5, 10R.

Self-efficacy. Self-efficacy is your sense of how well you are able to accomplish a task, and whether you have the skills and characteristics to be successful at it. The idea was pioneered by developmental psychologist Albert Bandura of the famous Bobo doll experiment. Whereas motivation is about how much or why you want to do something, self-efficacy is about your belief that you *can* do something. Like mindsets, self-efficacy influences how much you are willing to attempt a task and how quickly you will give up in the face of challenges. Unlike mindsets, self-efficacy is more of an assessment about yourself at a particular point in time rather than a general belief about how the world works.

Use the self-efficacy assessment for groups that struggle to overcome challenges or take risks. This assessment can be modified to reflect self-efficacy for specific projects or one's general work role. You could also evaluate self-efficacy to be a high-performing team, using the criteria from Chapter 2. Once areas of low self-efficacy are identified, discuss with the requestor whether it's best to target the problem areas with new skills training (if there is an actual lack of competency) or whether a team-building session focused on highlighting existing competencies would be beneficial. Some find it difficult to see their own strengths, so having the opportunity to be successful in a unique environment like an escape room can give clients a renewed sense of competence. As the facilitator, you can be mindful to point out the talents of your low self-efficacy participants.

Self-Efficacy Scale (Chen, Gully & Eden, 2001)

1. I will be able to achieve most of the goals I set for myself.

2. When facing difficult tasks, I am certain that I will accomplish them.

3. In general, I think I can obtain outcomes that are important to me.

4. I believe I can succeed at most any endeavor to which I set my mind.

5. I will be able to successfully overcome many challenges.

6. I am confident that I can perform effectively on many different tasks.

7. Compared to other people, I can do most tasks very well.

8. Even when things are tough, I can perform quite well.

Scoring: Take the average of all items.

Sense of community. Sense of community is about how much people feel connected to each other and how much they feel respected and valued by the group. People who feel disrespected or alienated from a group will not be motivated to spend time with their teammates and are generally less committed to the group's goals. Sense of community may seem unimportant and only of significance for "touchy-feely" types, but connectedness is a basic human need. Teammates who don't respect each other will undermine each other's work and ultimately be less successful. In the end, groups don't need to be the best of friends, but they do need to share a common commitment to the team's success and value the role played by each group member.

Use the sense of community assessment for groups that are experiencing interpersonal conflict or just seem to be not cohering. It could be that the feeling of disconnection is widespread or there are certain group members who feel alienated. If the entire group feels a lack of connection, then activities like concentric circles, goal setting, and visioning can build community. If certain individuals are not fitting in, activities like a task analysis or influence line can validate roles, and active listening or LARA can build communication skills.

Sense of Community (adapted from Deci et al., 2001)

1. I really like the people I work with.
2. I get along with people at work.
3. I pretty much keep to myself when I am at work.
4. I consider the people I work with to be my friends.
5. People at work care about me.
6. There are not many people at work that I am close to.
7. The people I work with do not seem to like me much.
8. People at work are pretty friendly towards me.

Scoring: Reverse items 3, 6, and 7 so that 1 = 5, 2 = 4, 3 = 3, 4 = 2, and 5 = 1. Then take the average of all the items.

Getting Feedback Afterward

As the facilitator, you will have some sense of how well the group met the learning objectives, but it is essential that you get direct feedback from the participants as well. At minimum, talk informally with a few participants or the requestor after the session. To get a better sense from everyone, you can distribute a feedback form with just two questions: what was beneficial, and what could have been improved? This will only take a minute to complete, and most participants are happy to provide comments. The feedback form can be given out immediately after the session (for the best response rate) or sent by email later. Use a longer feedback form if you are interested in analyzing specific aspects of the session or want to provide evidence of change in attitudes to the requestor.

Engagement

The Importance of Active Learning

This book is based on the principle of active learning, which is the idea that individuals learn better when they are active and engaged in their learning process. Sometimes lectures are an efficient way to convey information, but they also promote passivity, with students wanting to sit back and absorb. The best learning comes from when students have to question, extend, or otherwise engage with the material. Active learning doesn't mean that learning has to be "fun"— indeed some very difficult activities can be full of learning but no fun at all. Nevertheless, people do tend to enjoy active learning more than passive learning. Escape rooms are inherently active, but they do not always involve learning. You will have to create the learning through the activities and discussion around the escape room.

This book promotes active learning by giving you activities that require the participants to generate products individually, in small groups, and in large groups. Each format requires a different kind of interaction and pushes participants to think in different ways. You can better reach your learning goals by rotating through different levels of engagement throughout a session. Individually, a participant only has to sort out their thoughts and put them into a form that makes sense to them. In pairs, triads, and small groups of up to five or six, the social aspect is introduced. Participants have to make their ideas logical to other people and try to understand the ideas of others. At the same time, having the input of others can prompt participants to see their ideas in new ways or learn a new perspective. Participants also have to negotiate the social graces around turn-taking and listening to others. At the conceptual level, a small group's product should reflect the group consensus, but it will not equally represent each member's contribution. Since the facilitator is usually not part of the small group, it's harder to ensure that the group is on task toward meeting the learning objectives. It's usually beneficial to have a large group de-brief after individual and small group activities for this reason.

Large groups generally require a moderator to function well. A moderator can guide the content of the discussion as well as pay attention to group process: that is, whether everyone has the chance to participate and whether the group guidelines for respectful discussion are being followed. The large group offers the chance for each small group to share their products. This way the facilitator can determine progress toward the learning objectives and the other teammates can learn from more of their peers. The large group then offers the chance for the group to make broader generalizations about their work and to generate a finalized product.

To sum up, active learning is about emphasizing participants' engagement with material and providing different avenues for engagement. You won't find any lecture notes or PowerPoint slides in this book. Instead, all of the activities require the participants to do the work. As a facilitator, though, active learning requires you to provide just the right amount of structure to achieve the group's learning objectives—the activities cannot be completely open-ended. For each activity I give suggestions on how to structure the activity, but as you learn your own style you will modify them to fit. In the section on facilitation I will provide advice on how to effectively determine and implement your style.

In general, you should begin the session and each activity with a brief explanation of what is going to happen and what you want participants to get out of it. At the end of each activity and the session as a whole, you should summarize what you've done. You should also ask a few questions just to verify that participants got the point. You probably do not want to ask a very open-ended question like, "Does anyone have any comments?" because that could open the door to a whole new discussion. However, you do want to check in with participants and not just abruptly end.

Barriers to Engagement

Boredom. Everyone knows what it's like to feel bored: the activity at hand just isn't interesting or valuable to you. Unfortunately, in a mixed group it's impossible to know or play to everyone's interests. Some will be naturally drawn to puzzles and games. Others, usually the team leaders, will feel a deep need for the session and want to get the most out of it. Educational psychology Jacque Eccles and her colleagues have identified three aspects of interest that are helpful for thinking about boredom: interest value, utility value, and attainment value. Interest value is how an individual is intrinsically motivated to engage in the task. Is it something they'd do without being forced to? Those high in interest value are likely your escape room enthusiasts and gamers, and your main concern for keeping them engaged is having a high quality room. Other ways to build on interest value are to use activities that are inherently fun. Most people enjoy opportunities to talk to other people, to demonstrate their knowledge, or to use their creativity. During the session, you can extend the amount of time you give to activities that people seem to be enjoying the most, as long as you still have time to meet your learning objectives.

Utility value refers to how useful the activity is believed to be. Maybe your participants are not so sure about the puzzles, but they think the session will really help them work together better as a team. You've created enough perceived utility value in the requestor for them to use your services. To create and maintain the utility value during the session, you will need to clearly outline your learning objectives at the beginning of the session. Importantly, throughout the session you should highlight the learning objectives and how the group is meeting them. This can be done explicitly by asking participants what they have learned so far. You can also point out the growth you have seen in the group or individuals from one activity to the next. Participants who care about getting something out of the session will be looking for the feedback that they are indeed learning.

Finally, attainment value is about the importance of the task. Those high in attainment value care about the functioning of their team. The team's performance reflects on their competence as an employee or as a person who can successfully manage interpersonal relationships. Similar to those high in utility value, the best way to maintain attainment value is to draw attention to the team's learning objectives and how they are meeting them throughout the session. It's impossible to keep everyone interested at all moments, but by having clear learning objectives and a well-designed experience, you will minimize boredom.

Confusion. Confused participants quickly become bored or upset participants because they don't know how to re-engage in the task. Planning ahead is the best way to minimize confusion, but in order to reduce confusion during the session, you will need to keep an eye out for concerned expressions and an ear out for whispered questions. No matter how well you plan your activities and no matter how clear your instructions are, at some point someone will miss a key detail or misinterpret the instructions. Do not assume that participants will go to you for clarity. I've often found that participants who are confused about instructions will not ask the facilitator for help because they feel embarrassed. Another reason they might not ask because they could feel that if your instructions were unclear to begin with, you explaining again will not be useful. However, for some it's easier to understand directions when the facilitator is right next to them, holding the materials or rephrasing the instructions. So you should dispel participants' fears by making yourself available for help. Sometimes participants are not confused about instructions but are having trouble thinking through a problem. You as a facilitator can then ask some questions to help them work through it. A few minutes with an outside voice may be all it takes to get a group back on track.

Negative emotions and other participants. I'll discuss these barriers in the next section.

Other distractions. Other distractions can include room temperature, hunger, or life outside of work. You should strive to create as comfortable an environment as possible and make sure participants know that they can alert you about environmental concerns or the need for a break. As the facilitator standing in front of the room, you're somewhat disconnected from the experience of people who have been sitting down for an hour or more. I recommend a five to ten minute break every hour to an hour and a half as a rule. Additionally, research is clear that focus and attention are higher when basic biological needs are satisfied. Hunger and thirst in particular are big distractors that can be easily managed. Water and possibly coffee and other drinks are a must for sessions, but I also recommend providing snacks, especially for sessions over an hour or two. Most people will appreciate them, and those with medical conditions or the need to eat frequently will find them absolutely essential. Choose high protein, sustaining snacks like fruit or nuts and avoid those that will cause a sugar high and subsequent crash.

You as a facilitator cannot do much about participants who are distracted by life outside of work. All you can do is design a good session. If someone is consistently disengaged or seems upset but doesn't respond to your interventions, check in with the team leader or a co-worker who seems to be a close friend. As long as the participant isn't being disruptive, as described in the next chapter, you are safe to focus your attention on the rest of the team.

To sum up, the best way to encourage engagement is to design a session that maximizes interest value and meets the group's learning objectives. During the session, you should reinforce the value of the session and monitor the room for other concerns. In the next chapter I will describe the ways that participants can cause trouble and how to deal with each type of disruption.

Disruptive Participants

I define disruptions as things that cause unproductive sensations or emotions in the participants. Disruptions include participants being afraid to speak, being annoyed, or being confused about the current activity. Furthermore, it is important that participants maintain trust in the process and you as the facilitator, so disruptions also include anything that weaken that trust. Of course, it is impossible to prevent all disruptions, but you should minimize them as much as you can. This chapter describes the ways that participants create disruptions and the ways you can restore equilibrium.

Types of Disruptive Participants

Talkers. Talkers exist for a variety of reasons. Some people are more outgoing, just like to hear themselves talk, or believe their opinions are highly valuable. Others get very excited about the topic and find themselves with a lot to say. Some Talkers are people who think faster than the rest of the group. Responses come to mind quickly, so they are ready to share while everyone is still thinking. Thus, their opinions drive the conversation. Some Talkers are the office bully and seek to dominate others by being the loudest in the room.

At first, it might seem like a talkative participant is a blessing. Someone trusts what you are doing and is willing to talk! Unfortunately, the Talker, the participant who is constantly contributing, is more of a curse. First, the Talker can silence other participants because they may feel their smaller contributions are not as valuable. Some participants may have relevant insights but be afraid that they need to match the volume of the talker. Some may keep silent because they don't feel like there is enough time for them to share, especially in shorter sessions. They might be afraid of running over time if they try to fit their comments in alongside the Talker's. Other participants may keep silent because they are annoyed with the Talker. They think that by not responding to the Talker's points, they can move on to another topic of conversation, hopefully one that the Talker will not care about as much. By allowing the Talker to continue, you as the facilitator lose these participants' trust in your ability to provide a useful session. A talker can also drive the conversation away from your learning objectives by turning the conversation into their soapbox speech. Even if the Talker is making relevant points, you are the ultimate authority in the room and have the responsibility to uphold the group's guidelines.

As a facilitator, it's important to thank the Talker for their contributions but to remind everyone that they all have the responsibility to participate in the conversation. Sometimes a gentle reminder is enough to quiet the Talker. If it's not, you may need to be more explicit by asking, "Can we hear from someone who hasn't spoken yet?" If the Talker is someone who comes up with a response more quickly than the rest of the group, require everyone to spend a minute writing down a comment or two before you ask people to share. This allows the slower thinkers to catch up. Talkers who don't pick up on subtle cues might be best addressed on a one-on-one basis during a break. A more intensive intervention is to ask each person to make a comment before anyone can speak again, or to give each participant three to four tokens that represent a comment. Once a person is out of tokens, they have to wait for everyone else to use theirs before they get more.

Quiet Ones. Quiet participants exist for the exact opposite reasons that Talkers exist. Additionally, Quiet Ones may be bored or overwhelmed by negative emotions. You should be especially concerned when boredom or emotions are the reason, because both can prevent the participant from learning from the session. Then they are likely to give you a negative review because they didn't "get anything out it" or their particular issue wasn't addressed. At the same time, participants who feel negative emotions likely feel they cannot introduce their emotions into a professional conversation. It is important that you as a facilitator watch for nonverbal signs of boredom or emotion and invite Quiet Ones into the discussion. You can say something like, "I notice there are some people who aren't talking. Is there another point of view out there that we haven't heard?" You can check in with Quiet Ones one-on-one during a break if you are concerned about an outburst. If you get to the root of the negative emotion, you and the rest of the group will probably be able to resolve it. Boredom can also be caused by the Quiet One feeling that the group has missed a key point or is not addressing the "real" problems, in the view of the Quiet One. Even if the group is not able to resolve the particular issue, the group's positive response to the Quiet One can build a greater sense of community. Emotional conversations need to be carefully managed, of course, so I would direct newer facilitators to books on emotional intelligence.

Enthusiasts. You may have escape room enthusiasts, or budding enthusiasts, in your session. These participants can be beneficial because they are likely looking forward to the activities and their excitement might be contagious. On the other hand, enthusiasts can cause other problems. First, during the de-brief of the escape room they may want to spend a lot of time discussing the mechanics of puzzles or the storyline instead of shifting toward your learning objectives.

These digressions will probably seem irrelevant to the other participants. You can deal with this kind of disruption in the same way you would a Talker. Second, Enthusiasts may try to take over the escape room experience by telling the other participants what to do. This disrupts the natural character of the team, which may make it more difficult to draw connections between the team's performance in the room and their normal performance in the organization. It might also confuse participants about what they are supposed to "get" out of the experience or annoy the participants because the Enthusiast's directions might conflict with yours. If the experience in the escape room is unable to meet your learning objectives, your session will be less effective and you will lose your client's trust. Thus, you may need to take Enthusiasts aside to remind them that the experience is both for fun and for learning. If you see an Enthusiast taking over while the group is in the escape room, you might introduce instructions that require other team members to step up. You could even intentionally misdirect an Enthusiast who is too savvy about the room's mechanics, as long as you explain the reason for the deception later. Ideally, the Enthusiast will appreciate your skill at giving them a unique experience and meeting the team's learning objectives at the same time.

Turtles. Turtles are participants who are slow to "get it". In any learning setting people come in with a variety of background knowledge and cognitive abilities. In an ideal environment, learning can be tailored to each person's specific needs. Unfortunately, as a facilitator with a limited amount of time, you have to teach to the majority of the group. Therefore, sometimes you have to leave Turtles behind. The majority of the group will get bored or frustrated if you spend time repeating something they've already understood. It's better to sacrifice a few people than the overall group's learning objectives. Having a co-facilitator can be useful when you have Turtles because the co-facilitator can sit down with the Turtles to catch them up while you move on with the larger group.

Complainers. Complainers are those participants who don't value the session or aren't enjoying it and want to make it known. They are actually easy to deal with. After all, you know why you chose particular activities and what you want them to get out of it. The trick is delivering the explanation with confidence. You can also use the other participants as a buffer by having them describe what they find beneficial in the activities. If the Complainer is not convinced, don't get into a back and forth argument. Participants will attempt to take control of the session, but ultimately you are the one who has the responsibility to guide the group. You can ask the participant to talk with you later about their concerns and change the topic.

Space Alien. This is my term for the participant who says something that is completely "out there" and you have no idea where they are coming from. These are the moments that are most terrifying for a facilitator because there's no way to prepare. Sometimes you will just be surprised and have to take a few moments to recover. If you think further explanation might help, you can ask the participant to explain. Watch their teammates while they talk. If the participant commonly makes these kinds of comments, someone may jump in to help. Alternatively, you might see from the eye rolls that the others don't value the comments and you're probably safe to move on, too. You can always follow up with the Space Alien during a break. If you don't want to ask for an explanation and follow a participant down a strange road, you can say something like, "Thanks for that point of view" and transition to your next question or point. For the sake of the session, you want to spend as little time in a state of confusion as possible. You want to spend your limited time on discussion that will meet their learning goals. Participants will appreciate not going on tangents, as well.

To sum up, individual participants can be troublesome in their own way. Overall, it is best for you to be prepared by having a clear agenda and a clear idea of how to get to your learning objectives through discussion, which is discussed in the next chapter. Do not be thrown off by disruptions—stay positive and apply your interventions calmly and confidently. You are the leader of the session and responsible for (most of) what happens during it. Next, I will talk in more detail about facilitation style and what it means to have a positive and authoritative presence.

Your Facilitation Style

Tasks as a Facilitator

As a facilitator, you have three major tasks during the session: providing clear instructions, keeping participants on track in small groups, and moderating large group discussion. In order to provide clear directions, you will need to fully understand how the activities work and what potential points of confusion could occur. Before a session I usually sit down with my agenda and imagine each activity. How will I describe what the participants need to do? Where will the participants be sitting or standing? What materials are they using? How do they transition to the next activity? Often, this exercise will reveal holes in my planning. For example, once I was leading a panel and had planned for the audience to write down questions on index cards. Unfortunately, I had forgotten to put index cards on my materials list, so I had to ask a staff person to quickly find some. If you have employees or friends, it can help to do a run through of the instructions and transition points in the session.

When giving directions for activities that require some materials or set-up, it is usually best to give out the materials or do the set-up and then explain the directions. I have found that when you explain the directions first, participants get confused because they don't have the materials and they don't have a context for what you are telling them to do. Or participants will forget the directions in the time it takes to get set up.

Your second task is to keep the participants on track when they are working in small groups, both in terms of keeping track of time and of what participants are doing. Lots of learning can happen in small groups because people generally feel more comfortable and everyone has the chance to talk. At the same time, there is less responsibility to stay on task because the facilitator is not in control of the group. As a facilitator, you should rotate through the small groups while they are working to check for confusion or ways to help participants over road bumps.

You as the facilitator should also be listening for the tipping point when most groups are finished with the task. You might hear an increase in volume as more participants begin talking to their neighbors, or you will notice the conversations shifting to personal topics. Some groups will finish before others, and that is fine. However, you do not want the majority of the room thinking about irrelevant topics while you wait for slower participants to finish. The people who are finished will forget their insights from the small group work, and they might also begin to feel like the session is a waste of time if they can spend ten minutes catching up on each other's weekend. Usually a slower group will be able to catch up at another time. Even if they don't catch up, they will still learn from hearing the large group discussion, which will be more valuable for everyone than chit-chat.

The most important and difficult task as a facilitator is to moderate discussion. The next sections will give more advice on moderating discussion, but I will describe my overarching philosophy here. When I first began teaching, I was responsible for three discussion sections of twenty students. The professor assigned the students articles to read, and my role was to lead a discussion about the articles. I usually began my sections by asking "So what did you think of the articles?". When conversation lulled, I would throw out another question. This would continue for fifty minutes. At the end of the course, a lot of my evaluations said, "She doesn't teach. She just asks us what we think of the articles." I was confused, because I thought that *was* teaching!

Now I have a different way of leading discussions. In order to meet a team's learning objectives, it is not enough to merely invite conversation. Instead, you must have a clear idea of what revelations need to occur. For example, if the learning objective is to improve conflict resolution skills, then one of the revelations should be "the way I/we handle conflict is ineffective." As a facilitator, your task during the discussion is to prompt the statements that will lead to those revelations. The easiest way to do this is for you yourself to make the statement. You can bring up an example and tell a participant, "The way you handled that conflict was ineffective." However, most people will resist being explicitly told what to think. A more savvy approach is to have the statements emerge from the participants' conversation. What's important is that you don't have to rely on chance—you can structure your questions and prompts to lead to those statements and revelations. I think of this as the *path model of facilitation*: you have a path that you want to lead participants down. The path can be wide and allow lots of room for digression, or the path can be narrow and drive fairly quickly toward a particular point. The point is that you are directing the conversation. Since most of the comments come from the participants, they will feel that they generated the revelations, but you are not leaving the revelations to chance.

Here's an example. Jane is a team member who tends to take over tasks and push her co-workers away. They get frustrated by this but find it difficult to explain to Jane what she is doing. After all, she has good ideas and usually gets the job done. The team's learning objective in your session is to improve the team's working relationships. You are aware of the situation with Jane and want her to have the revelation that her behavior is problematic. During the large group discussion you might bring up a moment in the escape room when someone was working on a puzzle and Jane took over. You can start by simply asking, "What happened with that puzzle?" Jane or the other co-worker might explain. Even if they were successful with the puzzle, you could ask, "What might have been another way to approach that problem?" The pushed-aside co-worker then has the opportunity to explain their approach and why it might have worked. You then ask Jane or the group as a whole why they didn't consider that approach. You then follow up by asking the pushed-aside co-worker how it felt to also have a viable solution. The answers to these questions are not as important as the next question, "Do you ever have this kind of situation happen in your organization?" Based on that question, or with some additional prompting, the group is likely to generate other similar situations. You will target the ones involving Jane and ask the participants draw parallels between that work experience and what happened in the escape room. At this point, some participants will catch on and begin making general conclusions. If they don't, you can ask more explicitly, "How does it feel to have that experience over and over again?" or "How would you prefer for those situations to go?".

Don't worry if participants see what you are doing when you're leading them down a path. As long as you display sensitivity and your leadership is focused toward the team's learning objectives, the participants will respect your efforts to help them learn. Most people prefer a session that they get something out of, even if it seems a little forced. Only a very skilled moderator can make the path seem entirely self-generated.

The figure below illustrates the path model of facilitation, showing how the facilitator opens with a question and only follows up on the comments that are relevant to the path.

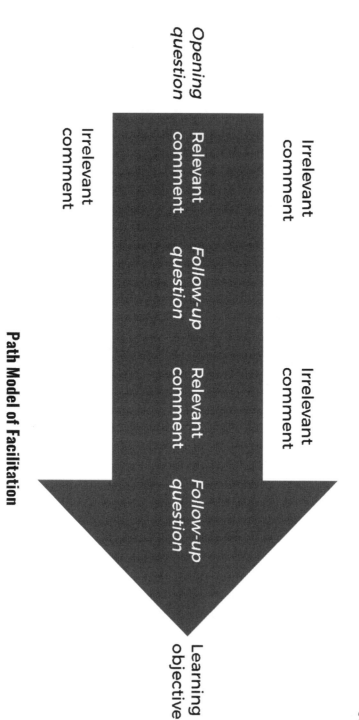

Path Model of Facilitation

Irrelevant
comment

Opening
question

Relevant
comment

Follow-up
question

Relevant
comment

Follow-up
question

Irrelevant
comment

Irrelevant
comment

Learning
objective

Another thing to think about when moderating discussions is that you are moving from specific to general and general to specific. What that means is that you start out with specific moments or experiences in the activity or escape room. Then you push the participants to think about situations or problems that were similar to that experience in order to help them draw general conclusions about themselves as individuals or a team. On the other hand, you are also moving from general to specific in terms of your path to the learning objective. You start out by inviting any ideas or comments, and you follow up on the comments that fit on your path, eventually moving toward a specific revelation. You should plan out your questions in advance so that you can have this structure and multiple ways to get down your path.

From Specific to General and General to Specific

Specific experiences

General questions

Timeline of Discussion

Specific learning objectives

General conclusions

Facilitation Styles

Every instructor and facilitator has their own style based on their personality and experiences. Your style as a facilitator might even be different from your everyday self. I personally am a relatively shy and reserved person, but in front of students I seem a lot more outgoing and expressive. Part of the difference that my enjoyment of teaching comes through, and part of it is that I've noticed students are a lot more responsive to my high energy self than my more laid back self. You will also have to develop your own style, but the next section will give some general outlines and pros and cons.

The Moderator. This is my facilitation style. I throw out a question and wait for responses. When someone responds, I nod or ask, "What do others think about that?" If the response is unclear to me or could be unclear to other participants, I ask for further explanation. I don't offer praise or comment on how interesting comments are. When a few people have spoken, I will ask another question that summarizes the previous comments and builds on them, leading the discussion further down my path. For the most part, I don't comment on every response and I encourage participants to have a conversation with each other rather than directing their comments toward me.

The benefit of this style is that it forces participants to take the lead in the conversation. Because I give little feedback on the appropriateness of responses, participants have to rely on the agreement or disagreement of their peers to continue the conversation. This style places the facilitator much more in the background; my shaping of the discussion is less obvious, so the discussion feels more natural.

The downside of this style is that some participants desire more direction. Some want approval of their statements, or they want the facilitator to express an opinion. If someone asks me for an opinion directly, I will give it, but generally I do not explicitly express my views to the group. They can come out in other ways, though. If a participant says something controversial or that I might want to challenge, I first ask for responses from others: "How do others feel about that?" Often times another participant will challenge the statement, and I can call for other responses along that line. If no one does, then I will step in to offer a challenge, usually in the form of another question, such as, "Do you think that's true in all circumstances?" As I discussed in the conflict section, it's never a good idea to get into an argument with a participant. A facilitator's job is to prompt learning, not lecture, so as a Moderator I see myself as providing opportunities for reflection but never forcing a thought. So, some may want more interaction from a Moderator, but I find this style effective for most participants.

The Commentator. This style of facilitator has a much more active role. They are more likely to respond after each participant's comment. The response could be evaluative ("That's interesting") or another question on the same topic. The conversation becomes more of a series of exchanges between the facilitator and one participant until the facilitator decides to shift focus.

A benefit of this approach is that it's easier to highlight important points or have one participant fully elaborate their thoughts. In the Moderator style, if the facilitator or another participant changes the topic, an insightful comment could be lost into the air. Another benefit, especially if you are short on time, is that you can more directly lead the participants down your path of discussion.

A downside of this style is that some participants are intimidated by it. They may be less likely to share if they know the Commentator will respond to them directly. It's also easier for a Talker to dominate the conversation because they can engage with the Commentator through several turns. At the same time, it's somewhat easier to manage the Talker because the response can be "Thanks, now let's hear from someone else."

The Devil's Advocate. A variation of the Commentator is the Devil's Advocate. This is the facilitator who sees it as their role to challenge most of what is said in order to extend the participants' thinking. Some participants thrive with this style, but it is very intimidating for many. You have to be very careful to not seem like you are forcing your views on the participants or arguing for the sake of argument.

A Positive and Authoritative Presence

Regardless of your particular style, you as the facilitator must maintain a positive and authoritative presence. By positive, I do not mean that you have to be overly outgoing or unnecessarily sunny. Instead, a facilitator should display confidence and model respect and trust. First, it is important that the facilitator seem competent so that the participants are reassured that you know what you're doing and can help them achieve their learning objectives. Second, facilitators must uphold the guidelines for discussion themselves and enforce the guidelines among participants. This means modeling respect and creating a supportive environment. For example, thank participants when they share a personal story or make an especially insightful comment. The facilitator should also demonstrate that they trust the participants to be engaged in the process and learn as much as possible. The facilitator should never write-off or denigrate participants—challenge them if appropriate, but never in a disrespectful way. The facilitator should also demonstrate trust in the process of team-building and the session you are leading. If you don't believe in what you are doing, why should the participants?

This relates to the second point: A facilitator must also maintain control of the session. By control I mean having a general hold over where the group is and where they are going, not micromanaging every moment or bossing participants around. In order to do this, you must pay attention to both content and process. Content is related to the learning objectives: what do participants need to get out of each activity, and how will your instructions and discussion questions get them there? You need to monitor throughout the activities and discussion to see where participants are and how to guide them. Process refers to the structure of the session—the way you give instructions, the nature of transitions, who is speaking when, whether the guidelines are being followed, the energy in the room, and environmental concerns like air temperature. Content should be at the forefront of the participants' minds, but you will need to manage the process in order to make that happen. Distracted participants will not get as much out of the session. Careful planning will help you with both content and process. During the session, you will need to pay attention at both levels: for example, what is this participant saying right now? (content) and how will I transition to the next activity after two or three more comments? (process). It is difficult at first but becomes easier with experience.

One aspect of control that new facilitators have trouble with is maintaining an air of confidence. May presenters begin by apologizing for some lack in their experience or the content, or during the presentation they will apologize for some perceived flaw in the materials. My advice is to never apologize for minor flaws, and smooth over any small errors in procedure. By apologizing, you first call to mind problems that the participants may have never noticed. Second, you undermine participants' trust in your ability to effectively help them reach their learning objectives. If you start by admitting what you don't know, why are the participants spending their time listening to you? Similarly, if you point out a minor flaw, participants may begin to wonder in what other ways you are unprepared. By all means, do apologize for major errors that disrupt the flow of the session, such as not having enough handouts. But apologize quickly and move on. Do not allow participants to dwell on your incompetence. Third, by positioning yourself as someone with a lack, you open the door for dominant participants to attempt to take over the session. Some people are more than happy to angle for a leadership position if you show weakness. Usually this will be the office bully or someone who does not see value in team building. If someone else is in control of the session, it is unlikely that the group will achieve their learning objectives.

Some new facilitators protest that they want to be honest and straightforward with participants. So why not tell the funny story of how you almost forget to pick up the coffee? My response is that if honesty interferes with the group meeting their objectives, it is not necessary. You only have a few hours to get to know the group and move them through the session. Your insecurities and need for complete honesty are irrelevant to that process. If you almost forgot coffee, what else has almost gone wrong with this session? Are you the right professional for this work? It is possible to share personal anecdotes and reveal your personality with undermining your position as the leader of the session. Instead of sharing a story that shows incompetence in your role, talk about something the participants can relate to, like a conflict over the coffee maker. You can even relate such stories to the participants' learning objectives, for example by talking about how you successfully resolved the conflict.

At the same time that you are maintaining control over the overall process, you should also recognize that you are not responsible for everything that happens during the session. You cannot force anyone to learn, and you cannot ensure that the guidelines are never broken. All you can do is maximize learning opportunities and respond to disruptions in a positive and authoritative way when they occur.

Some other things to pay attention to when facilitating are:

Your own reactions. You are human, so you will find some comments funny, confusing, or frustrating. It's fine to show your true reactions, but in some cases you may want to moderate your reactions to help the group. For example, showing frustration might discourage participants and cause them to disengage, but when conveyed in a positive manner ("I really think you all can get this, just keep trying!"), frustration could motivate participants.

Conflict is OK. Conflict will happen in many sessions, so you should learn to be OK with it now. You can prepare for conflict by imagining possible areas of objection and resistance during the session. Often, conflict is surprising, such as when an innocent question uncovers a long-standing debate between two people. How you address the conflict will depend on the group's learning objectives. If the conflict is relevant, you can try to mediate a conversation in the large group. You could also break the group into smaller groups with instructions to develop their points of view before returning to the large group. Be sure the guidelines for discussion are being followed. If the conflict is irrelevant or seems like it will go too far off-topic, you can ask for it to be tabled, and you can explain your reasons for doing so. You only have a limited amount of time with the group and there are certain objectives you need to achieve. Acknowledge the importance of the issue as you put it aside.

Groups have a process and individuals have a process. As a facilitator, you are most interested in how the *group* is performing. What is the level of energy? What's the dominant emotion? What do most people seem to be learning? However, groups of course are made up of individuals. You will thus need to do some monitoring of individuals, particularly if they are leaders, dominant, or an outlier. Pay attention to group leaders because they might have final say about how well the session went and whether to use your services again. They are also generally responsible for building on what happened when the group goes back to work. Therefore, you need to make sure they "get it". Pay attention to dominant individuals for a similar reason. They may be the loudest voices once everyone gets back to the office and could complain to the requestor or sway those who were fine with the session at first to their negative point of view. Finally, pay attention to outliers, the most and least engaged, because they can turn into disruptive participants. It would be great if you could pay attention at this level of detail to all participants (and it may be possible in very small groups), but your attention is limited, so focus on the potential sources of trouble.

Don't be afraid of silence. The biggest fear of most new facilitators is that they will ask a question in a large group discussion and no one will answer. Silence is not always a bad thing, however. Silence has many meanings: 1) participants are thinking, 2) participants are confused, or 3) participants are disengaged for some reason. The first is not a problem. The silence can seem much longer to the person in front, who is just waiting, than for the people who are doing the thinking. Advice I received about teaching is to count to 10 in your head. If participants still do not respond, you need to determine whether they are confused or disengaged. Confusion could be caused by an unclear question or by asking two questions at once ("What did you like most about the escape room? What did you dislike?"). Rephrase your question to be narrower and see if you get responses then. Disengagement can be caused by any number of reasons. You can diagnose disengagement through nonverbal behavior or simply by asking something like, "I noticed a lot of people seem checked out. Do we need to take a break?" You can address disengagement using the strategies in the disruptive participants section, by taking a five minute stretch break, or by having the group confer in small groups for a few minutes.

Plan your questions. You should use your learning objectives to plan a general set of questions for each activity and the escape room debrief. Appendix B also has a set question prompts that you can use during discussion to focus on different areas.

Working with Co-Facilitators

Co-facilitators can help you in many ways. They provide an extra person to pay attention to process and environmental concerns. Participants can build rapport with a second person if your personality does not quite suit them. You can also play off your co-facilitator's energy during the session. Additionally, co-facilitators can provide an additional authority in the room for participants who might be trying to take over the session. Your co-facilitator can be one of your co-workers or a member of the group you are working with.

Working with co-facilitators requires additional set-up, however. Of course, you must both be clear on the learning objectives and agenda. You should discuss how to divide up responsibility so that both facilitators have similar levels of responsibility, or at least clearly defined roles. Participants will treat the person who talks the most as the leader and the other person as the assistant, so pay attention to who asks questions during discussions and debriefings. You can have each person be responsible for one activity at a time or take turns asking questions. Also be aware of how your identities might influence participants' perceptions of you. For example, a male facilitator might naturally be assumed to be the leader, so you might decide to give the female co-facilitator a greater percentage of speaking time to offset this assumption.

Co-facilitators should also be aware of each other's style, strengths, and weaknesses. I was in a situation where I had a Moderator style and my co-facilitator was an extreme Commentator. We had a lot of hard feelings by the end of the session because I thought she was talking too much and she thought I wasn't taking on enough responsibility! If we had been more aware of our facilitation styles in the beginning, we could have discussed how to merge both of our styles or decide for one of us to take the lead during one discussion and the other to lead the discussion at a different time. By learning each other's strengths and weaknesses you can assign tasks accordingly. For example, some people are good at keeping track of time whereas others give especially clear directions. Be explicit with your co-facilitator about your expectations, your preferences, and the ways they can support you.

It is important that you maintain a positive and authoritative presence in regards to your co-facilitator, also. Discuss conflicts with your co-facilitator away from participants. If participants are aware of serious conflicts, they may lose trust in your leadership. The conflict might also open the door for dominant participants to try to step in. If your co-facilitator makes a mistake during a session, cover for them in the moment and either let it go or find a quiet moment to check-in with them. You want to show that you have confidence in your partner. If you absolutely cannot hide conflict or mistakes from the participants, model being a good team member and demonstrate good conflict resolution skills.

After the session, debrief with your co-facilitator about how things went and areas for improvement. It is important to be open and honest, but you may not need to discuss every minor flaw in the session. Like any team, you will want to focus on your goal: identifying that ways that you can be more effective in helping your clients achieve their learning objectives.

Conclusion

Thank you for reading this book. I've offered some general guidelines on how to design your team-building sessions, discussion of activities and assessment tools, and advice for leading activities and discussions. Facilitation is a fun and unique way to interact with your customers compared to giving a presentation or observing people in an escape room. You will learn a great deal about yourself through your interactions with other people. You'll also gain amusing insights into human nature and learn some fun facts along the way! Good luck and all the best with your business.

If you're interested in further developing your team-building services, please get in touch with me at christy@exitsantacruz.com. I can offer advice on developing your services and creating agendas for particular groups. I can also offer facilitation training for you and your team virtually or in person. Also get in touch if you're interested in having your participants take their assessments online rather than on paper. I can provide an online platform and personalized individual and group score reports. I love statistics, too, so let me know if you're interested in more complex analyses! Finally, you can download the assessment tools and handouts in this book from our website, www.exitsantacruz.com.

References

Adams, M., Bell, L. A., & Griffin, P. (Eds.). (2007). *Teaching for Diversity and Social Justice.* Routledge.

Button, S. B., Mathieu, J. E., & Zajac, D. M. (1996). Goal orientation in organizational research: A conceptual and empirical foundation. *Organizational Behavior and Human Decision Processes, 67,* 26-48.

Chen, G., Gully, S. M., & Eden, D. (2001). Validation of a new general self-efficacy scale. *Organizational Research Methods, 4,* 62-83.

Deci, E. L., Ryan, R. M., Gagné, M., Leone, D. R., Usunov, J., & Kornazheva, B. P. (2001). Need satisfaction, motivation, and well-being in the work organizations of a former Eastern Bloc country. *Personality and Social Psychology Bulletin.*

Dweck, C. (2000). *Self-Theories: Their Role in Motivation, Personality, And Development.* Philadelphia, PA: Psychology Press.

Dweck, C. S. & Leggett, E. L. (1988). A social cognitive approach to motivation and personality. *Psychological Review, 95,* 256-273.

Dyer, W. G., & Dyer, J. H. (2013). *Team Building: Proven Strategies for Improving Team Performance.* John Wiley & Sons.

Gillespie, P. (Ed.). (1999). *Love Makes a Family: Portraits of Lesbian, Gay, Bisexual, and Transgender Parents and Their Families.* University of Massachusetts Press.

Gosling, S. D., Rentfrow, P. J., & Swann, W. B., Jr. (2003). A very brief measure of the big five personality domains. *Journal of Research in Personality, 37,* 504-528.

Klein, C., Diaz-Granados, D., Salas, E., Le, H., Burke, C. S., Lyons, R., & Goodwin, G. F. (2009). Does team building work? *Small Group Research.*

Midgley, C., Kaplan, A., Middleton, M., Maehr, M. L., Urdan, T., Anderman, L. H., Roeser, R. (1998). The development and validation of scales assessing students' achievement goal orientations. *Contemporary Educational Psychology, 23*(2), 113–131.

Nicholson, S. (2015). *Peeking behind the locked door: A survey of escape room facilities.* White Paper available at http://scottnicholson.com/pubs/erfacwhite.pdf.

Rahim, M. A. (1983). A measure of styles of handling interpersonal conflict. *Academy of Management Journal, 26(*2), 368-376.

Salas, E., & Cannon-Bowers, J.A. (1997). Methods, tools, and strategies for team training. In M.A. Quinones, and A. Ehrenstein (eds), *Training for a Rapidly Changing Workplace: Applications of Psychological Research.* Washington, DC: American Psychological Association, 249-279.

Download PDFs of all appendices at

http://www.exitsantacruz.com/team-building-book

Appendix A: Handouts for Participants

Guidelines for Discussion

- Everyone should have the chance to share, and everyone has the responsibility to share
- Trust that everyone is doing the best they can
- Challenge the idea, not the person: focus on the content of what has been said, not on attacking the person who said it.
- Confidentiality: What is said here, stays here

Active Listening Instructions

In this activity you will practice your listening skills. Choose one member to be the talker, one to be the listener, and one or two to be observers. It doesn't matter who starts because you will all play each role. The facilitator will give you a prompt for each round.

1. For 5 minutes, the talker will speak about the prompt. The listener and observer should be silent.
2. For 3-4 minutes, the listener will repeat back what was said. Do not add to the information with your own thoughts.
3. For 5 minutes, the observer(s) will comment on how accurate the listener was and what they observed, including the listener's non-verbal behavior. They can also comment on what they heard the talker and listener say.
4. Rotate roles and repeat the process.

Conflict Resolution Styles

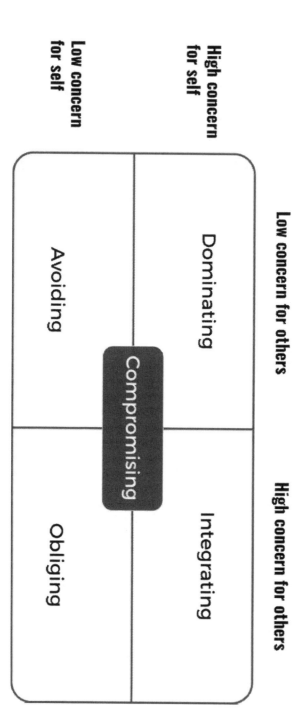

High concern for self

Low concern for self

Low concern for others

High concern for others

Dominating

Avoiding

Compromising

Integrating

Obliging

LARA Method

The following method can be helpful in seeking to understand others, dealing with challenging situations, and trying to find common ground.

Listen – Listen with empathy. Don't listen to form an answer. Allow the other person to speak freely about the issue at hand. Listen to find out what is at the heart of their message, what beliefs or values you hear in it.

Affirm – Repeat what the individual has stated. Find something in which you agree or find common ground and say so.

Respond – Make a response to the question/statement asserting your belief. Don't dodge the issue or talk around it –be straight forward.

Add Information –Provide additional information related to the content of the other person's thoughts, or raise a critical question to further explore the topic, with the aim of furthering dialogue (not necessarily changing the other person's mind).

Visioning

In this activity you will create a vision board. A vision board is a display that helps you imagine your goals and provide a visual cue that you can revisit on a regular basis.

The board can be anything you like, but here are some basic instructions:

- Think about your goals and your ideal future
- Give your board a theme, for example: "our vision for this organization"
- You can post images or words on the board
- Use images or phrases that are inspirational and that motivate you
- Focus on the positive
- Have fun!

Feedback Form

Thank you for spending time with us! We would like to get some feedback to understand how helpful this session was for you and your team:

What was the best part of the session?

What could have been improved?

Any other comments?

Appendix B: Assessment Tools

Goal Orientation Scale

Mark how true each statement is for you when it comes to your work.

	Not at all true 1	A little true 2	Somew hat true 3	Very true 4	Compl etely true 5
1. The opportunity to do challenging work is important to me.					
2. When I fail to complete a difficult task, I plan to try harder the next time I work on it.					
3. I prefer to work on tasks that force me to learn new things.					

4. The opportunity to learn new things is important to me.					
5. I do my best when I'm working on a fairly difficult task.					
6. I try hard to improve on my past performance.					
7. The opportunity to extend the range of my abilities is important to me.					
8. When I have difficulty solving a problem, I enjoy trying different approaches to see which one will work.					
9. I prefer to do things that I can do well rather than things that I do					

poorly.					
10. I'm happiest at work when I perform tasks on which I know that I won't make any errors.					
11. The things I enjoy the most are the things I do the best.					
12. The opinions others have about how well I do certain things are important to me.					
13. I feel smart when I do something without making any mistakes.					
14. I like to be fairly confident that I can successfully perform a task before I					

attempt it.					
15. I like to work on tasks that I have done well on in the past.					
16. I feel smart when I can do something better than most other people.					

Scoring: Take the average of items 1-8 for the mastery goal orientation score, and the average of items 9-16 for the performance goal orientation score.

Rahim Organizational Conflict Inventory–II

Please check the appropriate box after each statement, to indicate how you handle your disagreement or conflict with your peers at work. Try to recall as many recent conflict situations as possible in ranking these statements.

	Not at all true 1	A little true 2	Somew hat true 3	Very true 4	Compl etely true 5
1. I try to investigate an issue with my peers to find a solution acceptable to us.					
2. I generally try to satisfy the needs of my peers.					
3. I attempt to avoid being "put on the spot" and try to keep my conflict with					

my peers to myself.					
4. I try to integrate my ideas with those of my peers to come up with a decision jointly.					
5. I try to work with my peers to find solution to a problem that satisfies our expectations.					
6. I usually avoid open discussion of my differences with my peers.					
7. I try to find a middle course to resolve an impasse.					
8. I use my influence to get my ideas accepted.					

9. I use my authority to make a decision in my favor.					
10. I usually accommodate the wishes of my peers.					
11. I give in to the wishes of my peers.					
12. I exchange accurate information with my peers to solve a problem together.					
13. I usually allow concessions to my peers.					
14. I usually propose a middle ground for breaking deadlocks.					
15. I negotiate with my peers so that					

a compromise can be reached.					
16. I try to stay away from disagreement with my peers.					
17. I avoid an encounter with my peers.					
18. I use my expertise to make a decision in my favor.					
19. I often go along with the suggestions of my peers.					
20. I use "give and take" so that a compromise can be made.					
21. I am generally firm in pursuing my side of the issue.					

22.　I try to bring all our concerns out in the open so that the issues can be resolved in the best possible way.					
23.　I collaborate with my peers to come up with decisions acceptable to us.					
24.　I try to satisfy the expectations of my peers.					
25.　I sometimes use my power to win a competitive situation.					
26.　I try to keep my disagreement with my peers to myself in order to avoid hard feelings.					

27. I try to avoid unpleasant exchanges with my peers.					
28. I try to work with my peers for a proper understanding of a problem.					

Scoring: Take the average of each set of items—Integrating: 1, 4, 5, 12, 22, 23, 28; Obliging: 2, 10, 11, 13, 19, 24; Dominating: 8, 9, 18, 21, 25; Avoiding: 3, 6, 16, 17, 26, 27; Compromising: 7, 14, 15, 20.

Mindset

How true are the following statements?

	Not at all true 1	A little true 2	Somewhat true 3	Very true 4	Completely true 5
1. Everyone has certain amount of ability and we can't really do much to change it.					
2. People's ability is something about they that they can't change very much.					
3. No matter who someone is, he/she can significantly change his/her ability level.					
4. To be honest, people can't really					

change how capable they are.					
5. People can always substantially change how capable they are.					
6. Someone can learn new things, but he/she can't really change his/her basic intelligence.					
7. No matter how much intelligence people have, everyone can always change it quite a bit.					
8. Everyone can change even their basic ability level considerably.					

Scoring: Take the average of items 1, 2, 4, and 6 for entity mindset and items 3, 5, 7, and 8 for growth mindset.

Ten Item Personality Measure

Here are a number of personality traits that may or may not apply to you. Please write a number next to each statement to indicate the extent to which you agree or disagree with that statement. You should rate the extent to which the pair of traits applies to you, even if one characteristic applies more strongly than the other.

	Not at all true 1	A little true 2	Some what true 3	Very true 4	Compl etely true 5
1. Reserved, quiet.					
2. Extraverted, enthusiastic.					
3. Critical, quarrelsome.					
4. Dependable, self-disciplined.					
5. Anxious, easily upset.					
6. Open to new					

experiences, complex.					
7. Sympathetic, warm.					
8. Disorganized, careless.					
9. Calm, emotionally stable.					
10. Conventional, uncreative.					

Scoring: Reverse the items marked with an R so that 1 = 5, 2 = 4, 3 = 3, 4 = 2, and 5 = 1. Then take the average of both items. Extraversion: 1, 6R; Agreeableness: 2R, 7; Conscientiousness; 3, 8R; Emotional Stability: 4R, 9; Openness to Experiences: 5, 10R.

Self-Efficacy Scale

Mark how true each statement is for you when it comes to your work.

	Not at all true 1	A little true 2	Somew hat true 3	Very true 4	Compl etely true 5
1.　I will be able to achieve most of the goals I set for myself.					
2.　When facing difficult tasks, I am certain that I will accomplish them					
3.　In general, I think I can obtain outcomes that are important to me					
4.　I believe I can succeed at most any					

endeavor to which I set my mind.					
5. I will be able to successfully overcome many challenges.					
6. I am confident that I can perform effectively on many different tasks.					
7. Compared to other people, I can do most tasks very well.					
8. Even when things are tough, I can perform quite well.					

Scoring: Take the average of all items.

Sense of Community

The following questions concern your feelings about your job during the last year. Please indicate how true each of the following statement is for you given your experiences on this job.

	Not at all true 1	A little true 2	Somewh at true 3	Very true 4	Complet ely true 5
1. I really like the people I work with.					
2. I get along with people at work.					
3. I pretty much keep to myself when I am at work.					
4. I consider the					

people I work with to be my friends.					
5. People at work care about me.					
6. There are not many people at work that I am close to.					
7. The people I work with do not seem to like me much.					
8. People at work are pretty friendly towards me.					

Scoring: Reverse items 3, 6, and 7 so that 1 = 5, 2 = 4, 3 = 3, 4 = 2, and 5 = 1. Then take the average of all the items.

Appendix C: Forms and Handouts for Facilitators
Team-Building Request Form

Our team building sessions are 2.5 hours long on weekdays during the day (between 8am and 6pm). Your team will complete self- and team-assessments, play one of the escape room games, and then de-brief the experience. We will tailor the event to your group/'s goals and needs.

Requestor name:

Organization name:

Email address:

Phone number:

Estimated number of people:

Preferred dates and times:

Briefly describe your team and what it does:

Briefly describe your team-building needs and goals:

Thank you for your interest in our services! We will contact you soon.

Session Checklist

Materials

- ☐ Water and snacks
- ☐ Nametags
- ☐ Copy of agenda for each facilitator and team leader
- ☐ Handouts for activities
- ☐ Pens and markers
- ☐ Other supplies for activities
- ☐ Feedback forms

Session Overview

- ☐ Introduce facilitators
- ☐ Have participants introduce themselves (name, role, fun fact)
- ☐ Overview of agenda for the day
- ☐ Logistics: location of snacks and bathrooms, etc.
- ☐ Guidelines for discussion (2 min)
- ☐ Activity 1 overview
- ☐ Activity 1 _____
- ☐ Preview escape room
- ☐ Bathroom break
- ☐ Escape room
- ☐ Escape room debrief

- ☐ Activity 2 overview
- ☐ Activity 2 _____
- ☐ Re-emphasize learning objectives
- ☐ Wrap-up activity _____
- ☐ Fill out feedback forms

Useful Questions for Facilitating Discussion

EXPLORATORY QUESTIONS—Probe basic knowledge

- What do you think about _____?
- How does _____ make you feel?
- What bothers/concerns/confuses you the most about _____? What are some ways we might respond to _____?

CASUAL QUESTIONS—Open ended questions that don't require a detailed or specific kind of response

- What is your understanding of _____?
- What do you want to know about _____?
- What is the first thing you think about in relation to _____?
- What are some questions you have about _____?
- State one image/scene/event/moment from your experience that relates to _____?

CHALLENGE QUESTIONS—Examine assumptions, conclusions, and interpretations

- What can we conclude from _____?
- Does _____ remind you of anything?

- What principle do you see operating here?
- What does this help you explain?
- How does this relate to other experiences or things you already knew?

RELATIONAL QUESTIONS—Ask for comparisons of themes, ideas, or issues

- Do you see a pattern here?
- How do you account for _____?
- What was significant about _____?
- What connections to you see?
- What does _____ suggest to you?
- Is there a connection between what you've just said and what _____ was saying earlier?

CAUSE AND EFFECT QUESTIONS—Ask for causal relationships between ideas, actions, or events

- How do you think _____ relates or causes _____?
- What are some consequences of _____?
- Where does _____ lead?

- What are some pros and cons of
  _____? What is likely to be the effect
  of _____?

EXTENSION QUESTIONS—Expand the discussion
- What do the rest of you think?
- How do others feel?
- What did you find noteworthy about this comment?
- How can we move forward?
- Can you give some specific examples of
  _____? How would you put that
  another way?

HYPOTHETICAL QUESTIONS—Pose a change in the facts or
issues
- What if _____ were from a different _____,
  how would that change things?
- Would it make a difference if we were in a
  _____ society/culture?
- How might this dialogue be different if
  _____?
- What might happen if we were to _____?
- How might your life be different if _____?

DIAGNOSTIC QUESTIONS—Probe motives or causes

- What makes you say that?
- What do you mean?
- What led you to that conclusion?

PRIORITY QUESTIONS—Seek to identify the most important issue

- From all that we've talked about, what is the most important concept you see?
- Considering the different ideas in the room, what do you see as the most critical issue? What do you find yourself resonating with the most?
- If you had to pick just one topic to continue talking about, what would it be?

PROCESS QUESTIONS—Elicits satisfaction/buy-in/interest levels

- Is this where we should be going?
- How are people feeling about the direction of this dialogue?
- What perspectives are missing from this dialogue?
- Everyone has been quiet for a while, why?
- How would you summarize this dialogue so far?

- How might splitting into groups/pairs affect our discussion?

ANALYTICAL QUESTIONS—Seek to apply concepts or principles to new or different situations
- What are the main arguments for _____?
- What are the assumptions underlying _____?
- What questions arise for you as you think about _____? What implications does _____ have? (for _____?)
- Does this idea challenge or support what we've been talking about?
- How does this idea/contribution add to what has already been said?

SUMMARY QUESTIONS—Elicit syntheses, what themes or lessons have emerged?
- Where are we?
- If you had to pick two themes from this discussion, what would they be?
- What did you learn?
- What benefits did we gain today?

- What remains unresolved? How can we better process this?
- Based on our dialogue, what will you be thinking about after you leave?
- Let me see if I understand what we've talked about so far... What have I missed?
- Ok, this is what I've heard so far... Does anyone have anything to correct or add?

ACTION QUESTIONS—Call for a conclusion or action

- How can we use that information?
- What does this new information say about our own actions/lives?
- How can you adapt this information to make it applicable to you?
- How will you do things differently as a result of this meeting?
- What are our next steps?
- What kind of support do we need as we move forward?
- How does this dialogue fit into our bigger plans?

EVALUATIVE QUESTIONS—Gauge emotions, anxiety levels, what is going well or not

- Is there anything else you would like to talk about?
- How are you feeling about this now?
- What was a high point for you? A low point?
- Where were you engaged? Disengaged?
- What excited you? Disappointed you?

Adapted from The Program on Intergroup Relations at The University of Michigan

Post Escape Room Discussion Prompts

- What was your experience like?
- What was difficult? What was easy?
- Who solved X puzzle? What was your process?
- What was your goal when you were doing X?
- How did you figure out X?
- How did you make decisions as a group?
- How was conflict handled?
- What patterns did you notice in how your team worked together?
- I noticed X happened; what was going on there?
- What did you do well?
- What could you have done better?
- Did you personally feel like you contributed? What a barrier to your participation?
- Who was "checked-out" or didn't contribute as much, and why?
- How does what happened in the room relate to how you work in the real world?
- What lessons can you take away?

Appendix D: Sample Agendas

Agenda #1

Learning Objectives: Resolve conflicts and disagreements more effectively and promote trust within the team

Time: 3 hours

- ☐ Introduce facilitators (1 min)
- ☐ Introductions: name, role, and how you would describe your conflict resolution style (5 mins)
- ☐ Overview of agenda for the day (1 min)
- ☐ Logistics: location of snacks and bathrooms, etc. (1 min)
- ☐ Guidelines for discussion (2 min)
- ☐ Conflict resolution styles assessment (5 min)
- ☐ Discuss conflict resolution style in small groups (5 min)
- ☐ Large group discussion of conflict resolution styles (10 min)
    - o What was interesting or surprising?
    - o How do your styles play out on a day-to-day basis?
- ☐ Preview escape room (2 min)
- ☐ Bathroom break (5 min)
- ☐ Escape room (60 min)

- ☐ Escape room debrief (15 min)
- ☐ Active Listening (45 min)
  - o Prompt: How did your conflict resolution style reveal itself in the escape room? How effective was it? What are ways you can resolve conflict more effectively?
- ☐ Active listening de-brief (10 min)
- ☐ LARA (10 min)
  - o Introduce concept
  - o Role play with a recent conflict
- ☐ Conclusions: re-emphasize learning objectives (1 min)
- ☐ Wrap-up activity: what I learned (1 min)
- ☐ Fill out feedback forms (2 min)

Agenda #2

Learning Objectives: Develop a vision for the team and set goals for an upcoming project

Time: 2.5 hours

- [ ] Introduce facilitators (1 min)
- [ ] Introductions: name, role, and what you like to do for fun (5 mins)
- [ ] Overview of agenda for the day (1 min)
- [ ] Logistics: location of snacks and bathrooms, etc. (1 min)
- [ ] Guidelines for discussion (2 min)
- [ ] Visioning (30 minutes)
  - o Explain activity
  - o Work in small groups (15 min)
  - o Present boards (10 min)
- [ ] Preview escape room (2 min)
- [ ] Bathroom break (5 min)
- [ ] Escape room (60 min)
- [ ] Escape room debrief (15 min)
- [ ] Goal setting (30 min)
  - o Explain activity/team leader explanation
  - o Work individually (5 min)
  - o Work in small groups (5 min)

- Large group discussion (20 min)
- ☐ Conclusions: re-emphasize learning objectives (1 min)
- ☐ Wrap-up activity: Thank you's (1 min)
- ☐ Fill out feedback forms (2 min)

Agenda #3

Learning Objectives: Increase bonding and team commitment

Time: 2 hours

- [ ] Introduce facilitators (1 min)
- [ ] Introductions: name and role (3 mins)
- [ ] Overview of agenda for the day (1 min)
- [ ] Logistics: location of snacks and bathrooms, etc. (1 min)
- [ ] Guidelines for discussion (2 min)
- [ ] Concentric circles (4 rounds, 20 min)
  - o Prompts:
    - What do you like to do for fun outside of work?
    - What do you like most about your job?
    - Where do you think you will be in five years?
    - What do you value most about this team?
- [ ] Preview escape room (2 min)
- [ ] Bathroom break (5 min)
- [ ] Escape room (60 min)
- [ ] Influence line (5 min)

- ☐ Escape room and influence line debrief (20 min)
- ☐ Conclusions: re-emphasize learning objectives (1 min)
- ☐ Wrap-up activity: Thank you's (1 min)
- ☐ Fill out feedback forms (2 min)

Made in the USA
San Bernardino, CA
27 February 2018